Praise for *The Hollywood Approach*

"The job of a CIA operative is similar to this book's approach: it's a little glamorous and all about knowing your mind is your best weapon to achieve your goals."

VALERIE PLAME, former CIA operative and author of *Fair Game: How a Top CIA Agent Was Betrayed by Her Own Government*

"Kristina Paider has a brilliant idea: use the same strategies that screenwriters and movie producers use to make us love and identify with our favorite Hollywood stars to help people draft and craft their own real-life stories. *The Hollywood Approach* is more than a self-help book. It's a compelling memoir from a master storyteller."

LOUANNE JOHNSON, former Marine, protagonist of *Dangerous Minds*, and author of *My Posse Don't Do Homework*

"I have led the research into the brain science of story—how the human brain relies on story elements to make sense of, and to create meaning from, narrative and experience. Kristina Paider's book is a masterful and accurate application of that story science to the process of designing and scripting a life. Tightly and powerfully written, it is a delight to plunge into with a steady flow of pearls to find on each dive."

KENDALL HAVEN, story consultant, master storyteller, and author of *Story Proof: The Science behind the Startling Power of Story*

"I love this book; it's not a book but a continued inspiration for a life lived and yet to come."

KATHRYN BOLKOVAC, author of
The Whistleblower: Sex Trafficking, Military Contractors, and One Woman's Fight for Justice

"A perfect pairing of fact and feeling, Kristina Paider's *The Hollywood Approach* weaves together strategies for personal fulfillment and success from the big screen, her masterclass clients, and, most poignantly of all, from her own life. More than just breaking down the building blocks used by screenwriters to advance their characters toward their goals, Kristina anticipates our doubts and helps us uncover and overcome our toughest roadblocks. Written with the authenticity of a true friend, this book doesn't just provide quality advice and leave you to muddle through on your own. Kristina's voice is there, representing your greatest cheerleader, urging you forward and surrounding you with tales of countless others who were once right where you are and found a way to push ahead to realize their wildest dream. She reminds us to rediscover and explore our own personal stories while drawing insights from our silver-screen heroines and heroes. After reading *The Hollywood Approach*, I am convinced that I have the skills, tools, and vision to take on my next ambitious project—and I can't wait to get started."

SHAUNA HEMINGWAY, former ambassador of Canada to the Dominican Republic

THE HOLLYWOOD APPROACH

KRISTINA PAIDER

THE HOLLYWOOD APPROACH

Script Your Life Like a Hit Movie
and Live Your Wildest Dream

Copyright © 2021 by Kristina Paider

All rights reserved. No part of this book may be reproduced, stored in a retrieval system or transmitted, in any form or by any means, without the prior written consent of the publisher or a licence from The Canadian Copyright Licensing Agency (Access Copyright). For a copyright licence, visit www.accesscopyright.ca or call toll free to 1-800-893-5777.

Every reasonable effort has been made to contact the copyright holders for work reproduced in this book.

Some names and identifying details have been changed to protect the privacy of individuals.

Cataloguing in publication information is available from Library and Archives Canada.
ISBN 978-1-989603-55-0 (paperback)
ISBN 978-1-989603-56-7 (ebook)

Page Two
www.pagetwo.com

Edited by Kendra Ward
Copyedited by Steph VanderMeulen
Proofread by Alison Strobel
Cover and interior design by Fiona Lee
Cover illustration by Brian Tong

hollywoodapproach.com

*This book is dedicated to every person with
the audacity to wonder, "Can I really do this?"*

HELL, YES.

CONTENTS

Introduction: The Call to Adventure *1*

1 Be Your Own Hero *13*

2 Your First Big Yes *31*

3 Your Narrative Forensics *49*

4 Character DNA Part I:
Strengths and Assets *69*

5 Character DNA Part II:
Amnesia and Superpowers *87*

6 Character DNA Part III:
Flawesomeness *103*

7 Allies: The Force Multiplier *119*

8 Drink Your Antagonists' Tears *135*

9 Mentors and Models *151*

10 Annnnnd... Action *167*

11 Plot Twists and the Dark Night of the Soul *185*

12 The Supreme Ordeal *199*

13 Love Conquers All *213*

14 Bulletproofing *227*

Conclusion: Your Next Call *247*

Acknowledgments *255*

Selected Sources *257*

"As you move toward a dream, the dream moves toward you."

JULIA CAMERON

INTRODUCTION
THE CALL TO ADVENTURE

• • • • •

"Wait a minute, maybe
I can do anything."

JANIS JOPLIN

I **PEERED OVER THE** edge of the seventh waterfall, heart racing as I looked down at the aquamarine pool thirty feet below. Target position clear. Life jacket tight. Helmet secure. There was just one leap between me and the life-changing moment I was hoping for. Nerves tangled up like seaweed in my throat.

Just do it. This could be it, part of me said.

What if you kick the bucket? This could be it, the other part said.

It was June 22, 2013, on the North Coast, Dominican Republic, at 27 Waterfalls (27 Charcos del Rio Damajagua). I had hiked up a ridge for two hours, and the only way to get back down was to jump into the falls, one by one.

Normally, this would be my idea of pure awesomeness. But for the last ten years, I had been having increasingly debilitating panic attacks in the water. It started with a regular cliff dive in Capri. It happened again while surfing in Sydney. Scuba diving soon became out of the question—I could no longer put my face in the water. Later, I could go only into swimming pools, and only up to my waist. Then as far as my knees. The latest had been dipping one foot into my Los Angeles pool. The only plausible incident I could tie the panic back to was leading the rescue of two boys in a riptide in Mexico. Even though I got them out fine, most of the thirty people around that day had urged me *not* to go in after them. It's possible that the horror of these people trying to stop me from helping these kids seeped into my subconscious and jabbed at me through these panic attacks.

In any case, now, some thirteen years later, jumping into 27 Waterfalls was my self-prescribed, self-administered exposure therapy. Subtlety is not always my strong suit.

BUT ALLOW me to back up a little.

As a story analyst and screenwriter, my job is to dissect and calculate the exact moves that get a character from point A to point B in a plausible, authentic, and entertaining way. An armchair psychoanalyst, detective, and logistician, if you will.

Early into learning the craft of screenwriting, I got curious and began applying the same approach to my life. I'd ask, "If Julia Roberts were playing me in a movie with this scenario right now, what would she do?" This new perspective led me to different choices, actions, and outcomes.

Life started to take on a new direction. When I had a broken heart to mend, I went to Capri, Italy, on an island adventure. In my day job in marketing, I had high-profile success, then landed a four-month stint in London to replicate it. I earned a promotion, and was voted into a local leadership position and recognized by the media. Better health, better relationships, better career moves ensued. In my work and life, I used the storytelling tactics I learned at the universities of California, Los Angeles (UCLA) and Southern California (USC) and from Hollywood powerhouses. Instinctively, I knew anyone could benefit from these lessons. But would they want to? What would I share? And how? I began experimenting with work projects, staff, friends, colleagues—anyone who wanted to play along.

At the height of my corporate career, I was a senior VP of marketing and research for a $15 billion hotel real estate company working with global luxury brands. I moonlighted as a screenwriter, and ultimately moved to Los Angeles and continued my studies on the UCLA campus while working as a story analyst for a production company.

Before long, I had racked up experience with tens of thousands of scenes and thousands of characters. I would ask, "What is the decision and action that moves this character toward their goal? What stands in their way? What are the ultimate needle-movers to success?"

Real Life and Reel Life

We connect with Hollywood characters because we see our potential through them and in them. We feel their pain in "the dark night of the soul"—the moment when, after the heroine has kicked major ass toward her most daring dream, everything goes to complete shit and she has to figure a way out, up, and through—despite almost unbearable odds. We rally and we cheer her on as if our own life and future happiness depend on it. We are inspired, thrilled, devastated, and fulfilled through these characters' stories.

Movies inspire us. But it goes both ways. We inspire movies, too. This book profiles many stories of true heroines condensed in a less than two-hour sequence—a roster of concentrated decisions and actions that make for a great study when contemplating our own next moves.

We know that these infinite possibilities take place in real life as well as on-screen. We are the heroes and heroines, and they are us. You just may not be looking at it that way—yet.

Even though we may have different goals, backgrounds, ages, and needs, the factors that drive our stories to success are the same. Not similar. Not kind of like each other. Exactly the same. They all have it. Desire. Goal. Character. Strengths. Flawesomeness. Victories. Setbacks. Allies. Antagonists. Action. Plot twists.

The movement from one point to the next comes down to two things: choices and action.

My point A (deciding to attempt jumping into 27 Waterfalls to blow my panic attacks out of the water, literally) to point B (get into any pool, lake, or ocean panic-free) had nothing to do with fame, fortune, or wearing a cape and everything to do with the choices I made and the actions I took. I applied the same exact Hollywood story components from my script work to my real life. And you can, too.

The First Yes Is Only the *First* Yes

Saying the big yes to go to 27 Waterfalls was the first in a long list of yeses that led me to living my next wildest dream. And there were a lot of ups and downs. Once I got to the Dominican Republic's North Coast, I tried and canceled the trip to the falls three times. I extended my time on the island four times. In ten weeks in Cabarete, I had more friends than I had in five years in Los Angeles, and my screenplay was sent to Mark Wahlberg. I later moved to an oceanfront penthouse—heaven. I auditioned for a band, fell in love, started a writers group, worked as a guest chocolate chef, wrote my best screenplay, pivoted my career, upped my poker game, helped a friend get her recycled shoe and purse company started, co-led a flood relief operation, and had tremendous life adventures.

I've been inspired, I've conspired, and, heaven knows, in the tropical heat I've perspired. Sound awesome?

This is, quite literally, my wildest dream. What's yours? What's the craziest thing you can think of doing? Maybe when you really think about it, it makes more sense than you imagine.

Wherever you're at right now, like me, you did not come this far to come this far. I don't know your back story or your dark night of the soul, and I don't need to. Because I'm sure that you didn't arrive at this point to stay at this point. And before you begin this process, you need to know one thing: anyone can do this. More accurately, anyone can do their version of this. *You* can do this. *You* can live *your* wildest dream.

Approach The Hollywood Approach

In my Hollywood Approach master class, I walk students through the components of a protagonist's journey from a very specific point A to a very specific point B, just as we do in the movies. My students have rigorously tested the same exercises presented in the chapters of this book on their real-life goals. I have since developed and tweaked them for you to get the maximum result. At my students' request, I have included more of my personal story at the 27 Waterfalls to show you, step-by-step, the decisions, actions, victories, and mistakes I made to get to that goal—and the details of what happened then and since. You will also see dozens of movie examples with diverse characters.

The key concept is that information yields innovation. Therefore, I encourage you to do every exercise. Each one will help move your story forward. Consider the assignments as mental planks, if you will—you'll work parts of yourself you didn't even

"Life has no remote.
You have to get up and
change yourself."

ADAGE

know were engaged, and one day, voila, you'll revel in your newfound strength.

These concepts work as both a solo mission and a group adventure. My master class students are often surprised by how many similar themes they have among their goals, strengths, flawesomeness, resistance, actions, and insights. Many studies have documented the value of writing with a pen and paper, so I encourage that. Not because anyone's going to see it, but because writing it down has benefits for your brain's hard-wiring.

I invite you to create your life with even more intention, the way a creative professional—a screenwriter—does for heroes and heroines. This may mean getting "stretchy"—and considering your life, goals, choices, actions, strengths, and weaknesses through a new lens. You can do it.

Your Wildest Dream

I have this theory that getting to your wildest dream doesn't have to take very long. It doesn't have to be agonizing, as it was for me. I'm not suggesting you go at Mach speed with your hair on fire. But how about somewhere between Mach speed and lollygagging? I say that because having panic attacks in the water for thirteen years sucked. And it sucked *bad*. It was like being cut off from myself—even though I didn't recognize it for three years, was in denial for five, and was painfully aware for the other five. It wasn't until I had the fateful panic attack with only one foot in the pool that I zeroed in on the reality that I might be sentenced to sponge baths, or needing an exorcist, and took serious action.

Why did it take me so long? I'm not "shoulding" on myself, or anyone else, but I can't help but ask, should it have taken so much time? Could I have accomplished this sooner? If so, how?

This book is the answer to that, and to all of the other dreams we have on slow motion. Clarity and self-reflection will get us far, but we need more than that. This is a call to examine your life in a fun way—to name what you want and go after what makes you feel alive. It asks you what is worth focusing on and fighting for—like a heroine. "Happily ever afters" are not just for movie characters, they are for all of us.

Everyone can be heroic in their life. It comes down to your decisions and your actions. Just like movie heroines, we often don't change until the pain of staying where we're at overpowers the fear and uncertainty of something new.

I want you to live your wildest dream. Right here, right now, and out loud. And then your next one, and your next one after that. This is about engineering your current and future choices, actions, and plot twists so that you can claim your happily ever after, however you define it.

The Hollywood Approach works because it walks you through the same steps used to create a hero on-screen and has been road-tested and reverse-engineered for real life. You'll use the same tools, strategies, and tactics as

- Dorothy Gale in *The Wizard of Oz*
- Meg Murry in *A Wrinkle in Time*
- Rachel Chu in *Crazy Rich Asians*
- Debbie Ocean and her squad in *Ocean's 8*
- Wonder Woman
- Spider-Man, Iron Man, and Aquaman
- All of the lady bosses in *Ghostbusters* combined
- Every character in every *Rocky* movie
- Any other hero or heroine you can name

You can be as ready as these characters to achieve your goal.

If you are charting your path up, out, through, to, and/or onward, this book is for you. Let me show you how to use The Hollywood Approach to turn your next wildest dream into your reality.

BE YOUR OWN HERO

• • • • •

"I run my world."

BEYONCÉ

I**N THE SHOW** you call life, there is only one hero.
You.
You are the one who writes the scripts, calls the shots, celebrates victories, or regroups after defeats. Even if you are deferring decisions, "going with the flow," or following a pattern that was set up some time ago, you are still the hero of your story. Each day, you have the choice to continue the story you're in or pivot and start a new scene.

Our purpose is to evolve through our experiences. We don't need pills, patches, passes, pimps, proctologists, or prisons. We need to be our own hero. That's it. The problem is, being our own hero is not an exact science. Without a framework for it, how do we do that, exactly? Just... put on a cape? Climb tall buildings? Start tweeting or posting every time we see something that goes against our beliefs? What does it mean to be the hero in the show we call life? Hollywood has some great examples.

In my case, there was a lot I loved about my "show" for a long time. Career was good. Relationships were good. Health was good. I took risks and had grand adventures. But in 2013, something was nagging at me, and it became impossible for that thing to stay in the background any longer. It happened in a very specific, irreversible moment.

I was at my pool in Brentwood, California. Tom, my hilarious neighbor, was telling me about the meat fest of a barbecue spot he was opening in the neighborhood.

"I'll be sure to tell all my vegetarian friends," I said as I trepidatiously dangled my foot in our pool.

Oh shit. Oh shit. Oh sh—, I thought to myself. A stranglehold roiled in my throat. The panic shot up, and in an instant, I was suffocating. I yanked my foot back out. Too late. The ugly gasp was coming. Tom stared at me and everything went into slow-mo.

"I'm OK. Need... space." I gestured with my hand for him to stay put as I fought for breath. I crawled upstairs. I made it inside my condo, closed the door, and shut out the world.

It took the next hour to soothe myself back to a regular breathing pattern.

Air out... Fuuuck. Seriously? I only had one foot in the pool.

Air in... This was the worst one yet. But you've got this.

Air out... What's next, no soaking tubs?

Air in... Try not to think of anything.

Air out... How can I not freaking think of anything??

Air in... Stay calm. You can do it.

Air out... Wtf, I love soaking tubs and will not give them up!

Air in... Shit.

Air out... If I give up soaking tubs, baths will be next, and showers after that. And also, I can't let my niece and nephew see me like this.

Air in... Double shit.

Air out... OK, OK, OK.

Air in... This has to change.

Air out... Right now.

For the rest of the day and night, I was propped up with pillows on the couch, suffering the exhaustion of a marathoner sans the high. I was too baffled to cry. Too angry to let it go. Too stubborn to give up.

It was time to grab the reins of the show called life and to be the heroine of my own story. There was just one problem: I had no idea what to do next.

Except that maybe I did, kind of. I had written, created, analyzed, and collaborated on cuckoo protagonist situations before. Tens of thousands of them, actually. I'd gotten the hero out of a tight spot. Crafted a brilliant solution for a heroine's next action plan. Written the way to happily ever after despite villains, plot twists, and dark nights of the soul.

It was time to turn the focus on me and rise back up from this ten-year thing with the water. Not being able to put my foot in a pool seemed like bathtubs might be next and showers after that. Not being able to take a shower without a panic attack was as close to life or death stakes as I wanted to get.

Love Your Show

To begin this process, you need six things: yourself, a decent attitude, this book, a journal, a pen, and a goal—we'll get into more detail on that in a bit. These will be your tools of creation.

You are the creator, screenwriter, and heroine or hero of your own life. Right now, you may not always play it that way. But if you bring your inner heroine forward, condition yourself, treat yourself as the masterful creative force that you are, what else could possibly happen than the coolest life story—or best possible outcomes and experiences—ever?

Consider yourself a creative professional of your own life. For the duration of this book, commit to practicing the same rituals as successful Hollywood writers and see what kind of kick-assery you can create for yourself. Successful writers and other creatives routinely clear space, dedicate time, wear their lucky T-shirt, and orchestrate a very specific ritual of caffeine, treats, vitamins, and nutrition (strong body, strong mind) to open all seven regions of the brain and get the subconscious working for them.

You will need to have an open mind to try *this* particular recipe for results. You may not end up needing all the ingredients, so to speak, but I urge you to try them all on your first round through the book, and then adjust the recipe to suit your tastes later. You may find that some things—or combinations of things—surprise you, and that's why it's important to try everything and adjust later. Tune into it and mine it for information. Information is where the real power is.

You will need to open yourself up for new routines and practices. Not in the let's-do-CrossFit-for-an-hour-a-day kind of way, but in the let's-make-some-small-but-meaningful-adjustments kind of way. Clearing time and space to do the work regularly will help you get focus and rhythm. You'll want both: they will work to your advantage and help you accelerate results. Also, you owe it to yourself to dedicate your most powerful resources on a regular basis to go after what you really want in life. Focus will give you clarity. Clarity will give your dreams more power.

Channel Your Inner Protagonist

Fear not. This system works for goals of all sizes. If what you want is bigger than getting a hamburger tonight (there are most likely no major obstacles in that) and smaller than running for the next US presidency, I've got you covered. This system works great for large, complex, tricky goals that don't have obvious first steps in their action plans. It also works for goals you've gone for and fallen short on in the past. Maybe it's something you've given up on because it seemed too hard. Once you learn the concepts, you can apply them to virtually anything, but you may find The Hollywood Approach a bit over the top for something that doesn't have many obstacles in the way. So feel free to use this on the hard stuff: the goal that seems a little—or a lot—out of reach. The big kahuna. Or feel free to start with something smaller and use that as your training ground.

The rules of Hollywood storytelling are about managing information, making choices, and taking action. That's what makes it universal. That's why it applies to your life. One choice leads to the next set of circumstances, opportunities, and obstacles. Then the next, then the next. A film is a narrow window into a character's series of choices in getting from point A to point B. It's story in concentrated format: we don't see long periods of wallowing and indecision. There are no lag times. Why? Because no one's going to pay millions of dollars to produce that or invest two hours of their life to watch it. So screenwriting makes a great model to study.

Did you know that the average number of screenplay drafts completed before a movie starts shooting is thirty-three? Shocked the hell out of me when I first heard it, but it's true. So instead of around 110 pages for a single script, writers usually produce 3,630 pages to be whittled down. *On average.*

What if you auditioned thirty-three different solutions to a single problem? Say, the way you tackled a goal or dealt with a difficult boss, family member, or coworker. What if you put your energy into devising the best of the best solution for your biggest wishes and goals? What could be possible for you?

I don't care if your number one goal is up-leveling your entire life; transforming your company into a team of Jason Bournes who figure shit out and get shit done; overcoming a mystery health ailment to finally enjoy and thrive in life; or expanding your relationships and family. I don't care if it's starting a business or closing one; writing a novel; transforming your reactive attitude into a proactive one; launching a blog or vlog or travel podcast; or using your voice in a new way. Maybe you're starting an international culinary and yoga tour company or you want to ace your SATs so you can get into a great college, get a great job, and pitch in with your siblings to buy your parents a house.

Do the words "wild dream" instantly make you feel excited or overwhelmed? Does saying your dream out loud cause a lump in your throat or tears in your eyes because you've never even spoken it out loud before or because you want it so badly that the thought of failing is more than you can take? Do you feel that by not speaking it, you keep it in a safe space, away from failure?

I *know* you can do this. Whatever your "this" is.

I know because I've seen The Hollywood Approach work time after time in real life. It's easier and more fun than you can imagine. And every single example above is from one of my students.

Decide and Take Action

The two key components that determine your ultimate advancement toward a goal, or not, are choices and action. So if you know the factors that drive your choices and action, you have the information you need to choose differently and act quicker—which means you can engineer your success faster—if you want.

The problem for most of us is that when we figure out what we want to do and commit to it, we become so anxious about achieving results that we often fan out in too many directions. This dilutes meaningful progress. We put every iron into the fire

> **"There are no victims in this classroom."**
> LOUANNE JOHNSON
>
> ---
>
> In the 1995 biographical film *Dangerous Minds*, ex-Marine LouAnne Johnson takes a teaching job in a school with a group of tough at-risk students. She connects with them through unconventional methods like using Bob Dylan lyrics and karate. Ultimately, she helps them graduate and get into college.
>
> Portrayed by Michelle Pfeiffer, LouAnne starts out a little like a fish out of water but consistently sets the tone around the power of choice, even with extreme obstacles and the toughest of circumstances.
>
> Being a victim means succumbing to choices dictated by others or making passive choices—letting circumstances decide for you. The inflection point is when you can consciously make your own decisions. Then, you are being your own heroine or hero.

at the same time. We turbo-multitask. Instead, what we need to do is choose one thing to focus on and do that first. Then the next, and then the next.

You can spend less time in limbo and indecision just by looking at your problem—or story—through a different lens: that of your adjusted mindset. You can put your own physiology and biology—plus modern neuroscience—to work for you. You don't even have to memorize anatomy or impossible-to-pronounce medical terms. You can also make more strategic decisions, take

Movies are about actions.

Actions are about decisions.

Decisions are about information.

bolder actions, and craft more creative, workable solutions to achieve whatever you want—and have a freaking blast doing it.

Movie heroines and heroes teach us that with precise action, we can transform a situation quickly. Screenwriters are champions of character decision making. They have to be. They are responsible for achieving extraordinary character transformations in two hours: from an author to an adventurer, a teacher to a secret agent, a stutterer to a world-class speaker, a broke mother of three to a millionaire legal advocate, a trauma survivor to a legislative provocateur; from stage frightened and songless to rock star, broken-hearted to fulfilled, lost to found, devastated to hopeful, underdog to hero.

It can take weeks, months, or years in real life, but screenwriters get two hours—at best—to make this transformation real and believable. There is little time or production budget for characters to couch-surf, wallow, perseverate, complain endlessly about their plight. Watch any movie and you'll know. Therefore, screenwriters have to view characters and their choices in a specific way—that is, they must move the hero forward on their journey of transformation in a way that is logical and believable. Otherwise, we'd have movies with two scenes and no arc. Scene one: the character is broke, devastated, and desperate. Scene two, the character has the job and spouse of their dreams and has mastered the guitar, painting, or surfing on the side and just received a golden statue for their achievements. The End.

But that's not how it works, because that trajectory does not make an interesting film. Would you pay $15 to see those two scenes? No. They're uninteresting. Not compelling. They're flat-out boring and unbelievable. No one pays to see that. Film doesn't work that way. And neither does real life.

Yes, we have strengths and allies and brilliant moments of exhilaration. We also have flaws to overcome, obstacles to surpass, and plot twists to navigate. That is *real* life. And it is also *reel* life. The difference is, in real life, most of us don't hang out in an FBI war room/Hollywood screenwriting office/Office Depot shrine plotting our next moves on three-by-five notecards with colorful pushpins and strings indicating where we need to go next, *all* of the possible contortions to get there, and eight-by-ten glossies of the SWAT team of allies who will help us. Although we may have gallons of coffee and tea and piles of good snacks, we often don't have the mindset of a stealth squad of logisticians, strategists, and MFAs crafting our every move in the style and fashion of how we would most like to be living it.

Instead, we default-plan. Often only one time a year, at most, and without story meetings and a creation team behind us. That's not bad. But does that pattern lead us to our fullest potential? Are you living your wildest dream? You need to answer that question for yourself.

Screenwriters, as the people who craft the heroes and heroines on film and TV, are masters of information. They process the psychological profile of the protagonist against her ultimate goal and necessary resources, steps, and probable mess-ups inherent in the transformation to achieve that goal. The screenwriter anticipates every possible flaw, obstacle, and plot twist—and then executes the choices and actions in story form, architected with locations, costumes, props, and other elements to bring it all to life.

Being the master of your story, situation, and life, then, is about being the master of information.

Hard-Wiring in Your Favor

Now, although I said you don't have to memorize complicated anatomical stuff for this to work for you, I do want you to know that The Hollywood Approach is crafted to leverage your innate hard-wiring in your favor. Take, for example, the reticular activating system (RAS). Whether you've heard of it, could teach a class on it, or are still trying to pronounce it, it doesn't matter. It's a network of nerve pathways in the brain that connects the spinal cord, cerebrum, and cerebellum. Its job is to mediate the overall level of consciousness. In plain English: it filters out unnecessary information and lets only the important stuff through.

Entrepreneur says that the RAS, described as one of the most important parts of the brain, "influences cognition and is basically a filter for the roughly eight million bits of information (subconsciously) flowing through our brain. In other words, it eliminates the white noise."

What this means is that the more we keep our wildest dream at the forefront of our attention, the more our natural hard-wiring will work to bring it to reality. But it doesn't have to be our wildest dream or biggest goal. It can also be something as simple as... strawberries. Let's say we think about making a strawberry pie for a gathering next weekend, and we need to source strawberries. Suddenly, we start noticing the fruit everywhere—in a grocery flyer or in a neighbor's hands, or at a market or roadside fruit stand.

If you start thinking about a certain car in a certain color you want to buy, you will suddenly see it everywhere. Is it because there is a sudden influx of this car around you? No, it's because your RAS is working to make that connection. As it filters information from your conscious to subconscious, the natural hard-wiring in your RAS will work to make connections for you to achieve your goal, too.

This underscores the importance of the clarity of your goal, the past successes you recall, and how you visualize yourself achieving your current goal. When you have absolute clarity, your RAS will help you connect with the circumstances that will bring it to life. If your goal or your visualizations are vague, what you receive may be vague, too.

You Need a System

With the overwhelming volumes of information we consume regularly, you need a system to manage your decisions—a way to consciously choose what you're focusing on so that your RAS can do the rest. You need a way to filter what's relevant and continually harness your time and actions. Without your own personal management system, you are doomed to operate in default mode. Your life is better than that. Use the tools available to you and create your life like a masterpiece. Your fellow cast members will thank you.

The system used by Hollywood screenwriters and filmmakers is fearless, worthy of your time and attention, and easily applicable with some thought and consideration. Warning: it may change the way you watch movies from here on out... in a good way. One of my goals with this work is to make it so much fun and so effective that you can't help but absorb it, apply it, and adopt a new way of thinking—a fun way, one that gets you superior, inspiring results again and again. Throughout this book, I reference many different kinds of stories: fiction and nonfiction, public and private, funny and dramatic, famous and never-before-told. I also zero in on three films that are especially effective for personal story analysis and development: *Erin Brockovich*, *The Bourne Identity*, and *Akeelah and the Bee*.

Erin Brockovich is an Academy Award–winning film from the year 2000, based on the true story about an American legal-clerk-turned-environmental-activist, who, despite her lack of formal legal education, was instrumental in building a landmark case against the Pacific Gas and Electric Company (PG&E) of California in 1993. It stars Julia Roberts, and was written by Susannah Grant and directed by Steven Soderbergh.

The Bourne Identity is a 2002 American action thriller based on Robert Ludlum's novel of the same name. Jason Bourne, a man suffering from amnesia, searches for his true identity while a team of assassins from a black operation within the Central Intelligence Agency (CIA), is at his heels. It stars Matt Damon and was written by Tony Gilroy and W. Blake Herron and directed by Doug Liman.

Akeelah and the Bee is a 2006 drama about an eleven-year-old girl who participates in the Scripps National Spelling Bee. Akeelah Anderson must overcome her father's death, her mother's grief, bullying, and being the underdog against wealthier, more experienced kids with more resources. Keke Palmer stars with Angela Bassett and Laurence Fishburne; Doug Atchison wrote and directed.

These films show you the universal themes of finding your way, taking chances, overcoming obstacles, accepting your true self, becoming who you are meant to be, and ultimately improving your life. They represent different time periods, genres, and tone, and were chosen for their universality. I also chose them for their mix of characters' goals, themes, and for fun, with which we learn so much better.

This leads us into our first exercises. Enjoy.

EXERCISES

1. Choose a dedicated workspace. Declutter it. Get a notebook and pen.

2. Watch or rewatch the movies *Erin Brockovich*, *The Bourne Identity*, and *Akeelah and the Bee*. This book features many examples and teaching moments from these films, and all three are used consistently in the lessons throughout the book. As you screen the films, jot down at least five choices of each of the main characters that affect the course of their story. Notice how he or she opens or closes doors/opportunities as a result of where, when, and what they say yes to.

3. Begin a practice of operating as a creative professional. You are, after all, creating the show you call life, and you are the star. For the duration of this book, commit to practicing the same rituals as successful Hollywood writers—give yourself time and space to do the work, and nourish your body, mind, and spirit. Sign the "Heroine's/Hero's Power Contract" (provided on page 30) to commit to this process and yourself.

4. Meditate for a minimum of ten minutes on your goal—on your story—every day. Aim for the same time—as you wake or before you go to bed are two of the most popular times that work for my students. Better still, engage a friend or partner in the discussion of your goal and work.

5. In your notebook, record three key insights or observations from doing these exercises. These can be something that

stands out from screening the films and observing the hero/heroine's choices, how you felt about clearing space for your work, what it means to you to be the creative executive of your life, or anything that stands out as new, remarkable, or interesting. What surprised you? Perhaps it's the ease, effectiveness, how little or much time it took, what a difference a small action made, or something that seems both obvious and like a major revelation even though it's been right in front of you.

Heroine's/Hero's Power Contract

I, _____ , am fearlessly examining the ways in which I can call forth my inner heroine/hero.

I now make a sacred pact to accept myself as a powerful creator of my life and to move toward and live out my next wildest dream.

I understand that growth requires moving through new, possibly uncomfortable things.

I get that I may have to expand my boundaries.

I am willing to tap into my courage.

I acknowledge I am doing this for my greater good.

I reserve the right to expand this contract and give myself permission to grow through each step in bringing on my inner heroine/hero.

Signature and date

_____

YOUR FIRST BIG YES

• • • • •

"If you don't live your life,
who the fuck will?"

RIHANNA

I **WAS NOT IN** the mood for a wedding.

A client owed me $30,000. I was renting my Los Angeles apartment on Airbnb (*shhh*) and crashing at a soul sister's place to make ends meet. It had been almost five years since I left my job as senior vice president of marketing and research of a global hotel real estate company, and all I had managed to do was create an outpost of my old position: same work, same grind; plus, I had just published a book and was readying a screenplay for market on top of it. A colleague had taken to sending me morning texts as long as the Declaration of Independence. And following a bizarre series of events, the friendship with my soul sister melted down.

So, even though I adored my cousin Jackie, a ray of sunshine since the day she was born, I wasn't feeling "game" for a wedding in the Dominican Republic.

But then, the one-foot-in-the-pool panic attack happened. Days later, my landlord told me he was selling his condo—as in, the one I was living in and renting out on Airbnb. I had to move, and I was feeling done in more ways than one. After obsessively googling every possible variation of "how to overcome panic attacks in the water" and finding nothing, I received the third call from my mother to ask if I was sure I didn't want to go to the wedding. By that point, I did want to get out of town. So I started researching the Dominican Republic. If I used my preciously hoarded air miles to go there, what else was there to do besides frolic at an all-inclusive for five days?

And then, not even while thinking about panic attacks, I found it. A short, eight-hour bus ride from my cousin's wedding in Punta Cana. Cue the epic soundtrack music, angels' harps, victory buzzer, and stadium applause. There it was: 27 Waterfalls. A two-hour climb up. To get back down, you must jump in each of the twenty-seven waterfalls.

Something in me stirred. I was soul-certain that attempting this feat would lead to one of two things: cardiac arrest or blowing my panic attacks out of the water, literally. Two words sprang to mind: "exposure therapy." And then two more: "*hell, yes.*"

I booked the ticket.

The Sacred Call to Adventure

A call to adventure—aka your next wildest dream—can be a deep longing for a goal or experience to be attained. Or, like mine, it can be an unexpected event that causes a tailspin of consequences for which you need a strategy to catapult yourself to the other side. It can also be many, many things in between, next door, and around the corner. You can call it whatever you want, and as you can imagine, the bigger and juicer your goal or adventure is, the more exciting the rewards of pursuing it will be.

In the structure of a Hollywood movie, a call to adventure sets the story into motion. It is the heroine recognizing that a question needs to be answered, a challenge needs to be accepted, a goal needs to be conquered, a mission needs to be accomplished.

> **"There's more to life than being a passenger."**
> AMELIA EARHART
>
> ---
>
> The 2009 biographical film *Amelia* features pioneering aviatrix Amelia Earhart, portrayed by two-time Academy Award winner Hilary Swank, who bought a secondhand biplane and became the sixteenth woman in history to receive her pilot's license.
>
> Amelia was smart, resourceful, and ambitious. She set numerous records, including being the first woman to fly solo across the Atlantic Ocean, and the first person to fly over both the Pacific and Atlantic oceans.
>
> Amelia consistently bucked every convention that dictated the role of women. While the exact circumstances of her disappearance over the Bermuda Triangle remain a mystery to this day, what we do know is that she spent her life making conscious choices to pursue her dreams. Like Amelia, your first and early yeses to put yourself on the path of your dreams will allow you to start and gain momentum toward other yeses and key milestones toward your goal.

It's when the hero—um, *you*—says yes and commits to the path, no matter what. It's the saying of yes again and again.

- It's African American detective Ron Stallworth joining the Ku Klux Klan to infiltrate its Colorado Springs chapter in *BlacKkKlansman*.

"We don't turn to story to escape reality. We turn to story to navigate reality."

LISA CRON

- It's Laura Burney faking her own death to escape her abusive husband in *Sleeping with the Enemy*.

- It's the pampered Prince Akeem of Zamunda looking to find true love working at a fast food restaurant in *Coming to America*.

- It's Thelma and Louise taking off in the turquoise 1966 Ford Thunderbird on a girls' trip in *Thelma & Louise*.

- It's Whoopi Goldberg's Laurel Ayres inventing a male persona and cross-dressing in order to make it on Wall Street in *The Associate*.

- It's sugary sorority queen Elle Woods enrolling in Harvard to win back the boyfriend who dumped her in *Legally Blonde*.

- It's Frank "Tony Lip" Vallelonga, a rough-around-the-edges bouncer, agreeing to be the driver and bodyguard for Don Shirley, a sophisticated African American pianist, on an eight-week concert tour in the Deep South in the early '60s in *Green Book*.

To start out, you—the heroine in your own life—must first and foremost identify your goal and say yes to the adventure. To the thing you want. To your heart's desire, your lifelong quest, your big dream, your big moment.

Identifying the Call

Psychologists would say that people's goals—or calls to adventure—usually fall into three categories: health, relationships, and career/finance. Adventurers would think of goals in terms of travel, experiences, and personal challenges. Artists would claim their masterpiece, something that pushes their boundaries like never before or a new achievement as their goal. Parents may think of this as school, a part-time job, or household projects or sports for their child. If you are focused on finances, you may think of goals in terms of units sold, a promotion received, or a salary threshold attained. Extreme sports enthusiasts would define their call as the next highest peak, roughest waters, longest race.

The Hollywood Approach helps you orchestrate the heroics it will take to make your *big* dream a reality.

Many things can trigger a call to adventure. It can be a slow, deep longing from within that leads you to fulfill a life calling, as it was for Amelia Earhart before she set new records for her flights across oceans. Her calling began when as a child she first saw a plane in Kansas and knew she wanted to fly. Alternatively, the catalyst may be a sudden or dramatic change—for example, when covert CIA operative Valerie Plame's identity was leaked to the press by the Bush Administration in real life (and in the movie based on her life, *Fair Game*), she was propelled into the public eye and had to redefine her career and life, which has included penning a number of books and running for Congress. Your goal could be heralded by a slow rumbling, a to-your-core unsettledness beckoning for you to marvel at something, as experienced by Elizabeth Gilbert in her autobiographical book *Eat Pray Love*, which Julia Roberts brought to life in the film of the same name. Your call to adventure can be wanting to take your life to the next level, like Joy Mangano, the struggling mother of two and family caretaker who pursued the creation of her invention—namely, a self-wringing mop—and became a self-made millionaire, played by Jennifer Lawrence in the 2015 biopic *Joy*.

Like these real-life heroines, my master class students also carved out formidable goals:

- Sharon wanted to get her financial house in order as her vision deteriorated.

- After grieving the loss of her mother, Tasha wanted to expand her culinary yoga retreat in Marrakech.

- Carole wanted to scale her business.

- Gunnel, Francesca, Cheryl, and Stephanie all wanted to write their masterpieces.

- Mike wanted to create a management philosophy that becomes the standard for modern business.

- Annie wanted to overcome obesity—get in shape and lose weight.

- Jason left corporate America and wanted to start a thriving coaching business.

- Megan wanted to purchase her first investment property.

- Facing a career crossroads, Melinda wanted to decide whether to give her dream another shot or let it go.

- Sheila wanted to launch a new brand that helps women over forty find freedom in becoming an expat or world traveler.

Your call to adventure could be a million other things. It doesn't matter what it is—what matters is that it matters to you. Now, unlike life, movies are generally an hour and a half to two hours in length. In that time frame, the main character tackles one major goal. And while a lot of other things happen, including side goals and objectives, a film, for the most part, focuses on the one major goal—the "A" story.

Many of the stories highlighted in this book are based on real people, and we are complex creatures. There is no denying that. Although I mentioned earlier that you can use this process for a goal of any size, as long as there are obstacles to achieving it, The

Hollywood Approach works best if you focus on an "A" story—your big goal now. You can get to your side goals and objectives later. For the purpose of learning this process, please plan to home in on your current "A" story as a rescue helicopter would a flailing swimmer in the middle of the ocean. Focus, friend.

Once you learn this system, you will find that it applies to many, many other areas of life, and tackling future goals will be easier. It's like fast-forwarding through the muck and getting to the good stuff.

Craft a SMART Adventure

If you pay close attention, a leading lady's (or man's) goal is similar to, if not the same as, a SMART goal, commonly used in the business world in project management, employee performance management, and personal development. Super-practical and straightforward. SMART stands for

- Specific
- Measurable
- Achievable
- Relevant
- Time-bound

Marry the romantic notion of your wildest dream with some rubber-meets-the-road mojo from this acronym.

Crafting your goal with these criteria helps you clarify what you want and how you will measure your success, effectively ensuring more of it. For some people, this one step of spelling out their mission, timing, possibility, and specificity sets them on a slightly different trajectory from their current one, putting them on the path with much more likelihood of success. In the case of my panic attacks, I wanted to move the needle on their intensity. I defined "move the needle" as getting to a point at which I could comfortably get back in the water and continue to progress. In other words, my goal wasn't to eliminate panic attacks in one shot—that would be unrealistic, and unlikely, setting me up for disappointment, if not failure by giving up entirely. Rather, it was to change the situation enough that I could continue progressing on my own without dramatic exposure therapy tactics in the future.

This work of clarifying goals is not just important—it's mission critical.

Protagonists' SMART Goals

Let's look at how our Hollywood film characters' missions play out in SMART goal format.

Erin Brockovich
Specific: Level up her life by doing right by the families of Hinkley

Measurable: No longer eat fruit cocktail out of a can; win the lawsuit

Achievable: Unknown but believed to be possible

Relevant: Absolutely, for her, her kids, and the families of Hinkley

Time-bound: As fast as possible

Jason Bourne
Specific: Find his identity
Measurable: Identity found
Achievable: Unknown but believed to be possible
Relevant: Absolutely, for the hero
Time-bound: Before he is assassinated

Akeelah Anderson
Specific: Place in each next spelling bee to ultimately qualify for the national bee
Measurable: Yes, number of spelling bees won
Achievable: Unknown but believed to be possible
Relevant: Yes, it involves studying and learning
Time-bound: Based on the competition schedules

And here's the breakdown of my goal in SMART format:

Kristina Paider
Specific: Move the needle on my panic attacks enough to be in the water by myself again
Measurable: Yes, entering the water without having a panic attack
Relevant: For the safety of others and for myself
Time-based: Be panic-free in water before Europe trip with niece and nephew

NOTE: NORMALLY, I would consider "moving the needle" a vague goal, but since there is no Richter scale for panic attacks, moving the needle so that I could get back in the water without a panic episode was as specific as I could be. You may find the same thing with your goal. Just make sure you know what it will look, feel, and sound like when you've achieved it.

What is success to you? The more specific you are about the outcome you want, the more likely you'll hit the bull's-eye. Is "trying" winning? Is it taking the leap no matter what? Or is it more than that for you? A certain salary, exposing wrongdoing, collecting a number of passport stamps? Is it a feeling, justice served, blazing a new trail, or something—anything—different? Whatever it is, make it on *your* terms. Ultimately, in the big picture, Erin wanted to support her family. Jason wanted to find out his identity so he could move forward with his life. Akeelah wanted to win the national spelling bee. What's your thing? What do you want?

Resistance

Let's pause for a moment for the little voice you might hear in your head whispering things like "I don't know" or "this sounds like BS" or that in any other way makes you want to jam a bookmark right here and advance directly to a Netflix binge. If resistance comes up for you, I hear you. And I encourage you to feel it and the full range of all your feelings *while*—meaning *at the same time*—you keep plotting ahead.

Just as for me and every other character out there, your goal, your deepest desire, is vastly powerful. You are activating that power when you say it aloud and allow yourself to be heard by witnesses and supporters. Writing, speaking, and discussing your goal, especially in specific terms—SMART terms—turns up the volume of possibility full blast. Your path emerges. And all you need to know is the one next step. That is how powerful this work is. And while it may be tempting to jet off and rock your show after reading this chapter, I hope you will stay with me until you finish this book, because there are more tools that can make your success even faster and easier, and have much more upside than you ever imagined.

So even if your goal scares you and feels ridiculous, foolish, or impossible, please keep going right now. And while you're doing that, let me introduce you to Bill, who I'm guessing felt some of these things when he was first asked about his goal.

Even, and Especially, Our Wildest Dreams

"I want to play drums for Fleetwood Mac," Bill told me. Laughter rippled through the Turning Point shelter. I looked at Bill, one of fifty or so residents attending my life skills class. That night, I was guiding a goal-setting workshop to help the residents transition out of homelessness to secure a job and housing.

Bill folded his arms and gave me a pointed look, daring me to respond.

Mind you, I've spent years analyzing goals, obstacles, and characters and what makes them tick while writing, consulting, collaborating, and analyzing eighteen gazillion characters in a bajillion screenplays. (My fact checker wants you to know that, literally, this is tens of thousands of scenes in several hundred screenplays with thousands of characters.) Not to mention managing my staff with SMART goals for a $15 billion company. Not many of those goals were, I might add, half as interesting as helping this gent, Bill, pursue rock stardom.

"OK," I said. "Here's what we need to consider." I fired off a round of questions with a blast of enthusiasm.

- Do you already know how to play drums?
- How well do you know how to play drums?
- Do you know any Fleetwood Mac songs? Which ones?
- How well do you know them?
- Can you play each song's solo or solos?
- What if you got your shot to play with them onstage, but they weren't playing the songs you already know?
- Do you think you should learn more?
- How will you go about doing that?
- How will you connect with Fleetwood Mac?
- Will you need to travel to do it?
- What's their schedule like for the next six months?
- How many locations are driving or bus distance from LA?
- Are tickets available? Will you access the event with a ticket?
- How will you set it up?
- Once you're up there, do you want an encore? To be asked back? For more?
- How do you think you should go about that?

Notice how the answers to all these questions would help us define Bill's goal in SMART terms? However wild or outlandish your dream may seem to you, you can nudge it toward reality by treating it practically.

As he listened to me rattle off questions, Bill's eyes lit up. His entire demeanor, posture, and expression changed. I looked at the other shelter residents, half-amused, half-triumphant. I knew I had made a connection.

"What else should Bill think about?" I asked. The group was silent as their eyes pinballed around the room. "Or is this enough for Bill to arrive at the specific, measurable, achievable, relevant, and time-bound elements of his goal?"

Aha. Lightbulbs. What happened next, well, it's truly pretty awesome. Bill didn't say much that night, and I never saw him again. The following week, excited to hear about his progress, I was given a message instead. Bill wouldn't be in my class that night, or for the foreseeable future. He was rehearsing for an audition for a church band. He was resourceful and had arranged free space to practice, and the only night he had access was Tuesday. Bill had taken action. The questions I had fired off helped him get crystal clear on his goal, and that clarity led to a doable plan, which moved him into action.

I sent him a message back. "Bill, you passed. Don't stop thinking about tomorrow."

Anybody can be their own hero. They just need a framework.

EXERCISES

1 Craft your call to adventure in a SMART goal format.

   Specific: _____

   Measurable: _____

   Achievable: _____

   Relevant: _____

   Time-bound: _____

2 Define your successful ending. Keep in mind that some stories, like films, have multiple sequels. One way to frame this is to think about your next success and what that looks like; that way, it doesn't risk taking a connotation that it's your only future success or your one shot. It's just the next big(ish) thing.

3 Journal or meditate on the following questions: What does it feel like to look at your goal in this format? Does it seem more doable now? Can you feel it becoming a real possibility? Make sure it is specific. "ASAP" is not a specific time measurement. If you have trouble with timing, try flipping the SMART elements and starting with the next one, two, three, or six months. What can you comfortably accomplish in this time frame toward your big-picture goal? That can help ensure it is achievable.

4 What observations or lessons stood out to you while or after doing this exercise? What did you find most difficult about writing a SMART goal—the specificity, the timing, as many workshop participants do, or something else? Remember that all information is valuable. Continue to observe and not judge your experience.

YOUR NARRATIVE FORENSICS

• • • • •

"You asked me if I ever stood up for anything. Yeah, I stood up for my life."

TINA TURNER

DIANA WAS THREE credits shy of her master's degree.

Why? She flunked math. "I'm not good at it," she said. She walked away from her goal of getting a graduate degree and the investment it took her to get that far, and started applying for jobs. She was tired of white-knuckling her finances and wanted to start her career.

A restaurant hired her as a food and beverage manager. "After about a week or so, my boss told me I had to do the bookkeeping. I had no idea what to do," Diana told me. She was intent on keeping that job. Fancy suits, new Manolos, and paying rent were on the line. What did she do? "I went to the library, got a bunch of books, sat down, and figured it out."

She shared that in my master class. A fellow student, Claudia, from Colombia, turned and said, "Yeah, me too. One day, I just had to figure it out: sink or swim. When I became a music manager."

I hear variations of this story again and again. This is what people do. When we have the right amount of need and desire, we overcome our own internal challenges and beliefs. We do this in thematic ways throughout our lives. And maybe also when we are so sick of the status quo that we'll take new action we thought never possible. We are capable of much more than we know and give ourselves credit for—and with the right combination of circumstances, we can do anything. Sometimes, it helps to reflect and remind ourselves that we've already done exactly that.

Your Story MBA

Most of the world is on a steady diet of TV. According to *Variety* magazine, Eurodata released a study on the viewing habits of ninety-five countries. North America ranked highest in TV viewership, with the average daily viewing time per person of four hours and three minutes. Europe was close: three hours and forty-nine minutes. Asia was less, at two hours and twenty-five minutes. This does not include DVDs, Netflix, Hulu, Amazon Prime Video, or other streaming services. The pre–COVID-19 pandemic report said that figures have remained steady in the last twenty-five years despite increasing online content. Pre-pandemic, Nielsen's and other ratings companies' reports clocked the viewing average for some age groups at up to five hours a day and thirty-five hours a week for the United States, United Kingdom, Spain, France, Italy, and Australia.

Compare these numbers to the time a child spends in school up to the twelfth grade. Thirty-five hours a week in classes, minus lunch and gym. Plus, students have summers off. Also compare the figures to getting an MBA, or any post-graduate degree, for that matter. Every two years of average television consumption is like earning another MBA in story. If you're like the average person, since about 1995, you have received twelve master's degrees in story consumption. (Perhaps a multiple of that if you tuned in more while quarantined during the COVID-19 pandemic.) You—we—have become sophisticated story consumers, and that programming is largely influenced by Hollywood.

But I'm not here to talk about how we consume a story about Katniss Everdeen or James Bond. I'm here to talk about how you see yourself in pursuit of your own current goal—how you see yourself in your story. The question is: How will you parlay the value of your Story MBAs into how you live the show called life? Let's dive into your narrative forensics and see.

What Your Story Can Tell You

"Narrative forensics" is the term I use to refer to analyzing personal back stories, the way I would a film plot. Films present a condensed version of the sequence of decisions and actions we make in real life. If you look at your own story the way you would analyze a film, you can glean key insights into your motivation, tendencies, and proven personal success patterns, and then apply them to the current situation. My master class students are often astounded by their discoveries, which yield insight into the internal driving forces they had forgotten about or that had receded over time. Analyzing past success stories will reconnect you with what makes you tick. When reignited and applied to your current goal, they become a force multiplier. Meaning, the personal knowledge of what motivates you—what propels you, what stalls you, and what stops you—creates more power for you.

Important neuroscience geek-out moment: the brain processes images sixty times faster than words, and our subconscious mind works a thousand times faster than our conscious mind. You're going to tap into that. Those facts are just the tip of the iceberg when it comes to the science behind why story is such a powerful tool. When you program your mind—in other words, consciously choose the success stories and imagery you have on a constant loop—you create and reinforce your own neurocircuitry. Cool, right?

Architecting a Hollywood Story

Screenwriters are the architects of Hollywood stories. A screenwriter's job is to create the blueprint—to map out the feature film from start to finish. This blueprint is called the screenplay, or script; it is approximately 100 to 120 pages, running between 90 and 120 minutes on-screen.

Timewise, a movie experience is less than one-third of that of an average book, which equals about six to eight hours of reading. That indicates what ninjas screenwriters have to be in conveying a lot with a little. They are masters at getting the most out of every action and decision. The screenplay sticks to two things: what is seen and what is heard. Everything else that the screenwriter writes and the protagonist portrays must evoke the emotions for the desired outcome.

This is a very close match to the experience of our external world. When we focus on our actions and words, our results reflect it.

The $13,513.51 Line

When I started film school in the late 1990s, I analyzed the budget for a big-screen film of $69 million. With this budget, *each page* represents a production value in excess of $500,000. Each screenplay page has some fifty-five lines. In many cases, that's around thirty-seven lines of text plus eighteen lines of spacing.

At $69 million, that was thirty-seven lines for a half-million dollars—which equals $13,513.51 per line in production value.

I share this not to underscore money but to highlight the thoroughness of the development process and, ultimately, investment in a single line of a Hollywood screenplay. There is no room for a single wasted scene, much less action, gesture, or word. Every line of action, description, and dialogue must move the story forward, convey new information, and entertain the audience. Now, do they always succeed? Of course not. Some are high points and some, bombs. Just like the moments in our lives.

Writing for Hollywood is as much a scientific and mathematical discipline as it is an art form. A couple of years into classes with my professor Robert Powell, I learned he was an ex-Air Force cop with black belts in both jiu-jitsu and aikido. That explained so much about so much. To say that his editing style was like working with Mr. Miyagi is an understatement.

Robert taught me the discipline of mastering every element of story to get the most out of each action and decision in the script. This involved acing every nuance of character psychology, being laser clear about motivations, honest about weaknesses and flaws, and carefully crafting the decisions so that the heroine could go from where she was to where she wanted to be. And so that she could navigate all the obstacles and antagonists she met along the way. That is the job of a Hollywood screenwriter. I also learned so much about life, and how every decision and action leads to the next one.

It is this art and science of screenwriting that I want you to apply in your life. What would it be like if you invested the same value and consideration in key moments of your life as a screenwriter does in a single line?

The Logline

To get started, let's define story from the screenwriter's perspective. The basic Hollywood story structure should reference a feature film's framework in a single line—the logline:

1. A character, who
2. wants a goal
3. and must overcome specific obstacles in order to
4. achieve that goal.

There are, of course, other elements. But the main character, goal, and obstacles are the absolute must-haves of a logline, and of a story. These elements define the journey on which the hero or heroine embarks. They convey a ton of information in a single line. And you now know the value and influence of a single line. Let's return to our three films—*Erin Brockovich*, *The Bourne Identity*, and *Akeelah and the Bee*—to take a closer look at this basic architecture of story.

Erin Brockovich

1. A story about a high-potential, unemployed single mom (character)
2. who wants to up-level her whole life (goal)
3. and must overcome her frustration, past choices, and lack of legal education (obstacles)
4. in order to become the underdog advocate she is meant to be (achieve that goal)

The Bourne Identity

1. A story about an amnesiac with special forces training (character)
2. who wants to recover his identity (goal)

3   and must overcome flashbacks, assassins, and zero information (obstacles)
4   in order to find out who he really is (achieve that goal)

Akeelah and the Bee

1   A story about Akeelah, an eleven-year-old with an affinity for words and language (character)
2   who wants to win the spelling bee (goal)
3   and who must overcome bullying, lack of resources, and no family support (obstacles)
4   in order to qualify for the national bee (achieve that goal)

Cracking Your Narrative on Past Success Stories

You can use the same formula to crack your narrative forensics and, ultimately, your success franchise.

The actions and decisions you've made in past stories can be applied to your goals in the present and future. Next, you'll put three of your past success stories into the Hollywood story structure to start mapping your own story forensics and drilling down to the absolute core elements of your past successes. You'll identify the turning points in your past successes and mine your own examples for information about your strengths and assets that can be used in pursuit of your current goal.

More often than not, my master class students are delighted to remember something they'd long forgotten—proof of their own badassery. This exploration unveils insights that propel them forward on their current goal. I wouldn't call it magic, but it sure feels like it, and the students definitely have what Oprah would call an "aha moment."

Every success story starts with a goal.

Let's turn the spotlight on you. You are going to name your past success story and write it out in the basic Hollywood logline format. Just as movies have titles, give your story a title and follow the structure of (1) naming and describing you in that story, (2) stating what your goal was, (3) identifying obstacles you overcame, and (4) stating your end goal/accomplishment. Past success stories you might tap into could be:

- an educational milestone like graduating from high school or university or passing a difficult course;
- a career milestone like landing your first job or promotion;
- an artistic milestone like a first or best performance, a visual or culinary achievement (your first mac and cheese); or
- a sports or physical achievement.

Your mission is to pick three past success stories. Stories from any time in your life are welcome, and those from your childhood or teenage years are encouraged. Sometimes, when we have more perspective—in other words, more years between now and the incident—it's easier and/or feels safer to assess our challenges and flaws, as well as identify our real victories. Pick some great stories. This is going to be your *success trilogy*. We will refer to these stories throughout the book and the exercises, so choose some gems where you learned and grew.

For this exercise, your goal could be any of the above or something else. Make sure you faced obstacles. What you *don't* want is something like "(1) I tried to make a chocolate cake, (2) I bought the ingredients, (3) I put it together, and (4) voila, I had a cake."

Annie was a master class student who wanted to overcome obesity and get fit. At first, she became so overwhelmed by the idea of facing her lifelong struggle with weight that, after declaring her goal, she freaked out, afraid that it was too big. In writing the simple bullets from her past success stories, Annie recalled one example in which she put herself in a specific time frame to achieve her outcome. She realized that this technique has consistently worked for her over many years in many situations. This is the kind of observation or insight we are looking for in our exercises at the end of each chapter—these small, insightful elements that when added together can change the trajectory for you as you move toward your goal.

In a second past success story, she declared a big goal to the world (or at least to her world). The public declaration was her commitment to opening up the door for people to check in with her about her goal along the way. And in a third one, Annie rediscovered that she has had numerous past successes by putting a gentle structure in place. In other words, she created a doable program.

Her next task was to figure out how to leverage her insights and apply these same elements to the context of her current goal of losing weight. She had already cut out sugar for six years and hadn't lost a single ounce. She decided to commit to a particular thirty-day cleanse. The specific time frame—a thirty-day window—forced her into a new discipline that she believed in because of her past success. This certainty amped up the specificity and achievability (or even perceived achievability) of her goal. Only in movies do we need to write heroes who take on impossible tasks. In real life, let's put the "A" in achievable.

For your best outcome here, choose stories in which you were challenged. They can be about something you did well, something that surprised you, something you didn't want to do, or something you had to do. They must be about when you took action, whether big or small, over a short or long period. This step is *critical* to your path. As you write your personal success stories in this format, *observe. Don't judge.* Just notice the obstacles both in and outside of your control, your internal and external factors, and keep moving. You are gathering information.

Pivot to Your Current Story

Next, we'll examine who are you in relation to your current story. Confident, shy, bold, reserved, underdog, overzealous, broke, rich, weak, ambitious, over-ambitious? This creates a container, or a canvas, for your current story. By clarifying who and where you are today compared with who and where you want to be, you define the arc—in other words, the size and scope of your endeavor.

This can lead to insights and validation such as, "Oh, no wonder this seems huge—it is," or, "When I put it this way, it seems more doable than I thought." Or it might be something in between. In any case, it will help prepare you for filling in the steps ahead.

For now, recall the goal you mapped out in SMART format from your work in chapter 2. What's your starting point? And what's the stated end—your end point? Plot both. State your goal in the Hollywood story format, which shows your arc, your change, your transformation. Let's look at Annie's, for example. Notice how she named it something meaningful and fun. Do the same. Make it flamboyant, something you want to return to.

Annie's a Secret Ninja

1 This is a story about a hard-working, at-her-wit's-end-about-her-health woman (character)
2 who wants to punch obesity in the face (goal)

3   and who must overcome her frustration about the lack of insight from the medical-industrial complex and six years of no results (obstacles)
4   to become the fierce and fit mama she's meant to be—and to stay with her wife and son longer (achieve this goal).

So, you will have your goal and your three past success stories stated two ways: in SMART goal format and in Hollywood logline format. The first will give you absolute specificity and clarity. The second will give you a simple way to state your goal in a single sentence and repeat it in a story format that aligns your past successes with your future victory.

> "I am not checking out. I need to change... I want to go someplace where I can marvel at something."
>
> ELIZABETH GILBERT

When the external trappings of success left Elizabeth Gilbert feeling disconnected and that she was not on the right path for herself, she decided to reimmerse herself into her own life with an epic trip to Italy, India, and Indonesia to rediscover her curiosity, inspiration, and appetite for life.

Julia Roberts has the starring role in the 2010 film *Eat Pray Love*, based on Gilbert's journey. Her quest for self-discovery emulates the narrative forensics required to uncover who you are and reconnect to what is important for your life and future.

Let's check in on Annie. Because of her insights and actions, she lost twelve pounds, even before the thirty-day challenge was over. This was after hovering at the same weight, to the ounce, for six years. She says she knows it's a long road—big dreams often are—but she doesn't fear the road. She also says that a lot has happened in these twelve pounds: walking became easier. Stairs became doable. Driving became more comfortable. Her confidence improved. What a way to start a journey.

Making Jambalaya

On a journey to a big goal, there will be things you don't know. Or things you *think* you don't know. Start with what you do know. I have a little mantra I say to myself when I'm tackling a big venture: "Go with what you know." Don't get caught up in perfectionist mode. It's bullshit, anyway. Give yourself permission to have a messy page with words crossed out and written over each other. This is a process and takes time to develop, percolate, and materialize.

This is personal, makeshift forensics; it's kind of like cooking. Think of making jambalaya in a slow cooker. It doesn't happen in five minutes, but action by action, you chop the vegetables, you pour in the stock, you peel and devein the shrimp—step by step, you get there. One tomato more or less isn't going to make or ruin your dish, and the exact amount of onion or paprika you use may not be calculated as you keep adding to it. It's like that here, too.

Feel a little lost, as if there are holes in your storyline or things that just aren't quite awesome yet? Don't worry. The important part is that you've taken the shrimp and vegetables out of the fridge and the spices out of your cupboard, and you've started.

Go at your own pace and trust the recipe. It worked for Elle Woods and Rocky Balboa, and it'll work for you.

Control Your Narrative

Story works on a subconscious level—and as you know, your subconscious mind works a thousand times faster than your conscious mind. The problem is, most people do not always consciously choose their actions in their own life story. If you're not consciously choosing, you're missing out on a *major* opportunity to *control your narrative.* You can use the knowledge from your twelve Story MBAs to visualize this in action. It's like when:

- Rocky drinks raw eggs and punches frozen meat as part of his training regimen for his once-in-a-lifetime chance at the heavyweight title.

- Daniel LaRusso paints a fence, sands a deck, and waxes a fleet of vintage cars to master the fundamentals of karate under Mr. Miyagi's guidance in *The Karate Kid.*

- Veronica navigates an unfamiliar world of dirty politicians, criminals, guns, and blueprints to pull off a $2 million heist to settle a debt owed by her late husband in *Widows.*

- Ferris Bueller fakes a sick day, tours Chicago in a sports car, sings in a parade, and contemplates life in *Ferris Bueller's Day Off.*

- Professor Melvin Tolson teaches a team of student debaters that in their time of racial inequality in the 1930s, words are their weapons. He coaches them through how to think, speak, punctuate, and pause, honing their debating skills to challenge Harvard in the national championship in *The Great Debaters.*

- Katniss Everdeen volunteers as a tribute to take her sister's place in *The Hunger Games*, where she sharpens her archery skills, fakes a love story with her partner, and fights for her life.

Minerva Mirabal was a law student graduate and an activist who controlled her own narrative. She and her sisters Patria and María Teresa, all married with children, helped organize and grow the underground movement that challenged Rafael Trujillo's dictatorship regime in the 1950s Dominican Republic.

The controlling regime continually tried to suppress anyone who stood up against them, but the sisters risked their lives to work in the resistance and were repeatedly arrested for their activities. Ultimately, Minerva and her sisters died for their cause. On November 25, 1960, the state murdered them for their part in trying to overthrow the government. The public outrage over this ultimately led to Trujillo's assassination six months later.

Although this might not seem like a happy ending to Minerva Mirabal's story, her commitment to a cause bigger than herself, her refusal to live by the state's rules, and her insistence on scripting her own narrative was instrumental to her dream and legacy. Almost two decades later, in the late 1970s, the Dominican Republic began transitioning to democracy.

The Butterflies, as the Mirabal sisters are known by Dominicans, became symbols of both democratic and feminist resistance. The International Day for the Elimination of Violence against Women, on November 25, was named by the United Nations in their honor. The wonderful book *In the Time of the Butterflies*, by Julia Alvarez, and the film of the same name are historical fiction accounts of the story of the Mirabal sisters.

Raise the Stakes

"Raise the stakes" is a phrase you'll often see in script notes or hear in writers' rooms. Its purpose is to urge the writer to push the protagonist to their limit to reveal their true character and increase the conflict.

That's not to say that everything is meant to be "life or death," as in the example of the Mirabal sisters. Raising the stakes can also be a figurative death, the elimination of a choice or opportunity, or a move toward the less favorable option. When we make our goal the center of our world, it can seem very much like life itself. And not getting that goal, when it's fully zoomed in, can appear or feel like a huge loss or figurative death. Raising the stakes can be the motivation we need to create real change—to move the needle toward the ultimate big-picture success of our goal.

EXERCISES

1 Write three of your personal past success stories in the Hollywood one-line structure.

   [Name of Story]

   1 This story is about _____ (character/you)
   2 who wants _____ (goal)
   3 and must overcome _____ (obstacles)
   4 to _____ (achieve this goal).

   We will use these three stories for analysis for the rest of the book, so don't close this session without scribbling something down.

2. Write these same three past success stories in SMART format.

   [Name of Story]

   Specific: _____

   Measurable: _____

   Achievable: _____

   Relevant: _____

   Time-bound: _____

3. Rewrite your current goal from SMART format into this Hollywood story format. Now that you've analyzed your past stories by breaking them down in SMART format and Hollywood story format, let's also "translate" your current goal (which you already have in SMART format from the last chapter) into the simplified, one-sentence Hollywood format, so you have the shorter version, too.

4. In your notebook, record a key lesson or insight from each of your three stories and your current goal. This can be anything that stands out to you as new, remarkable, interesting, or otherwise noteworthy. Notice if the insights tell you anything useful about how to approach your current goal or future work.

CHARACTER DNA PART I: STRENGTHS AND ASSETS

• • • • •

"I'm tough, I'm ambitious, and I know exactly what I want. If that makes me a bitch, OK."

MADONNA

IT'S LATE, AND RAINING. Jessica scans her 2,200-plus friends on Facebook to find the ones currently online.

Not him... not him... not her... there. This one. She goes to his profile and clicks the phone icon. "Hi... Sorry to call you so randomly like this via Facebook. Do you remember me from—"

Click.

She searches again, finds someone else, and clicks the phone icon.

"Hi... yes... it's been such a long time... no, we met in Barcelona in '05."

Click.

And again. "No, I wasn't the hot one, I was the little fat friend. Er... the funny one."

Click.

You may think this is a scene from a new Bridget Jones movie. But nope, it's real-life Jessica's account of what it was like to contact people she hadn't spoken to for ten and twenty years, including two people whom she might have slept with but wasn't sure. Eventually, she reached a guy whom she met at Borrowed Time, a beach in the Philippines.

"Yes. Yes, I know. I went off with the other guy. But you know, listen, please, hear me out. I'm really... I just wanted to ask you about something."

She'd made over thirty calls before she reached Theo.

Only days before her phone "campaign," she had stayed in bed on her birthday, immobilized with grief. Usually the life of the party, if not also the host, on this distinct birthday, Jessica took no phone calls, drank no champagne, ate no cake. A couple of days before, she had received the "final blow" from her doctor. Following two years of feeling unheard and being underdiagnosed and misprescribed for an extreme illness, she was told she needed a medication that in her country costs $900 a month. In other countries, it's $90, and still others, it's $3. Her doctor refused to do anything but insist that she pay her country's fee. That medical visit ended with a plea to not send her to a slow death.

She had reached her breaking point: the cakeless, guest-free, bed-bound birthday. But after she broke down, she broke through, with creativity, verve, and a flair that is uniquely, hilariously, heart-warmingly Jessica.

It turns out that Theo, the guy she met in Borrowed Time, was a registered psychiatrist located one direct flight away from Jessica's home city. When she told him what she needed, he said, "Absolutely no problem. I can prescribe. Yeah." So she planned the trip, staying in communication with him the whole way. In one message, she confirmed to Theo, "We've bought our flights, arranged for a hotel." They would be arriving the following Tuesday. Theo bristled at the "we-ness" of it all. Jessica clarified that she would be arriving with her boyfriend.

Suddenly, Theo ghosted. He wouldn't answer phone calls or return texts. But the tickets were bought and Jessica's boyfriend convinced her to go anyway. From that point, she sent a series of cheerful texts to Theo:

"Hi, Theo, we're on the plane, about to take off. See you soon!"

"Hi, Theo, we've arrived and are excited to see you."

"Hi Theo, we've just checked into the hotel. We're here just for tonight. Hope to see you soon!"

"Hi Theo, we're heading out to grab a bite. We leave tomorrow. Please let me know how to connect!"

Crickets. Crickets. And more crickets.

Jessica and her partner did what came naturally. They went out and got blistering drunk. They drank the sad. Drank the failed plan. Drank the deep, deep sorrow. After the alcohol sufficiently numbed them, they returned to their hotel and found a James Bond-esque text: "Meet me at such-and-such café in the next town over, tomorrow at 11."

But Jessica had reached another breaking point. The emotional roller coaster was too extreme—she had to get off. She shut down. Hit the wall. Couldn't bring herself to do it. She was unwilling to get her hopes up once again. But Michael, her boyfriend and a hostage negotiator by profession (I am not making this up), convinced her to go to the café in the next town to meet Theo. She acquiesced.

They arrived early. Jessica drank copious amounts of coffee. She ate copious amounts of pastries. Fifteen minutes went by. Then thirty, then forty-five. And then... a weird bike rolled up and a giant person unfolded himself and walked toward the door. Before he could reach to open it, Jessica sprang outside, wrapped her arms around him, and burst into tears. Surprise, relief, and gratitude surged through her.

She emotionally relayed her painful and debilitating journey over the last two years. How she had no energy, rapid weight loss, extreme brain fog, and hadn't been able to work or do much, and how she felt as if she were barely living because of this rare thyroid condition. Theo gave her the prescription and informed her about the number of refills allowed. And he told her one more thing: from then on, she'd be a registered psychiatric patient in that country. Oh, Jessica! Never a dull moment.

The Heart of the Story

Characters shape the heart of every story—fiction or nonfiction, successful or disastrous, victorious or defeated, rational or intuitive, fun or devastating. When we know who the heroine is and what she wants, we are on board with her journey. Who a person is and what they want are the first two components of writing a film. They are also the two key components in attracting and connecting with an audience. We see who she is, with her strengths, assets, flaws, weaknesses, and we understand her goal—so much so that we recognize parts of ourselves in her.

While some of us can relate to Jessica's story, not everyone has the particular strengths and attributes that make her who she is. Heroines have many character traits far beyond the scope of any story, but what we want to zero in on are the strengths a character exhibits, in context, that propel her toward her specific goal: in Jessica's case, her determination, creativity, and willingness to take unconventional action. Maybe others have similar experiences, but only Jessica can live, and ultimately tell, this story, this way.

Go deep beneath the surface and do the work to understand the elements of your character and what drives you. I want you to be reminded of what you're capable of, and to name it and claim it. Only you can be you.

You Are the Protagonist

In film, the protagonist's role is to drive the story forward. To do this in real life, *you* need to be clear on your goal, how you show up in your story, and *you* need to drive the action. You need to be clear that your goal may be slightly different or even way off base if you compare it to your friend's, colleague's, sister's, mother's, spouse's, boss's, kids', or dog's goal.

What do you want? What do you *want*? What do *you* want?

From information comes innovation. And *new ideas*. Remember that you are gathering information about a wide variety of aspects of yourself. Be kind to yourself and look at yourself with grace. Observe and notice what is available for you to learn. Do not judge. It will not help you.

Across the board, my master class participants report that they sometimes find some uncertainty around their next goal, and that's because they don't know all the pieces yet. If you have that experience, too, my counsel is to keep going. That's exactly why we're here. Trust the process. The clarity will come.

When I was trying to overcome my panic attacks in the water, I had no idea what to do or even how to frame it. I just knew that my goal was to not have them, so that if I was ever in a rip current situation or something like it and was the only one willing to help, I would be able to. So I just kept trying a million different things. Not until I got super-clear about what I wanted next, which was to move the needle on the panic attacks enough so that I could breathe in the water, did I identify the option of pursuing the (self-prescribed) exposure therapy of jumping into 27 Waterfalls as a viable solution.

But initially, ten years prior to the Dominican Republic trip, my goal had been to prove I wasn't having panic attacks. Then, when I realized and accepted that I was actually having panic attacks, I wanted to get rid of them. Finally, when the severity of the attacks increased exponentially, I changed tactics. Before that, I thought I could somehow "cure" myself in one fell swoop. After ten short years, I realized nothing was going to happen quickly. So my first step needed to be to override whatever was making the panic increase—I needed to blow up the circuit board on the panic attacks. In other words, I needed to move the needle on the severity of the attacks so that I could comfortably get back in the water.

I knew if I could do *that*, I could ultimately get back to swimming.

Story's Three Most Important Elements

What's the difference between an epic movie franchise and Oscar nominations and movies that get bumped off-screen, never to be heard of again? It's the same combination that turns ideas into visions, leaders into visionaries, goals into manifestos. The three critical elements of story are:

- Character
- Character
- Character

That's right. Character, character, and character. Think about it: there is no justice for Hinkley without Erin Brockovich, no Bourne franchise without Jason Bourne, no record-breaking national spelling bee championship without Akeelah.

If you watch Erin Brockovich closely, you see that she was technically already a legal rock star in the first fifteen minutes of the film. She just didn't know it, and she hadn't aligned with the

> "Doesn't matter who I work for,
> I wouldn't let anybody get away with this."
>
> KATHRYN BOLKOVAC
>
> ---
>
> Kathryn Bolkovac was a Nebraska cop who served as a peacekeeper in post-war Bosnia, hired to protect the law where lawlessness had run rampant. While at her post, she discovered a wide-reaching sex trafficking scandal involving military officers and diplomats—the very people who were meant to bring back order to Bosnia. Kathryn risked her life to bring the victims to safety and outed the United Nations for covering up the sex trafficking scandal.
>
> The 2010 film *The Whistleblower* stars Rachel Weisz as Kathryn. "Doesn't matter who I work for, I wouldn't let anybody get away with this," she says. This line reveals her character strengths: courageous, doesn't take BS, and committed to justice—a total badass. Just as Kathryn's strengths nudge her toward her mission, you too have qualities that, when put to the test, will help you overcome extreme obstacles and antagonistic forces.

circumstances to fully actualize herself. One day, she shows up in Ed Masry's office and simply starts working. Then she negotiates the crap out of a job, leaves him an out, and goes on to seek justice, against *every possible odd*, for the people from Hinkley. And why? Her actions were in her character DNA.

You also have character DNA, and cracking it is vital to your story. Because there is no story without you—you are the hero. You drive the action. You make the decisions that move your story forward, bring you closer to your goal, keep you stuck, move you away from your goal, or change the route to your goal—which can ultimately move you forward. No one else but you will make your story a success... or a future success. Or a non-story.

DNA Deep Dive

To better understand how to drive your story forward, you need to dive deep into your character DNA, looking at three key things in your past success stories:

1 Your starting point, or how you showed up in your story
2 Where you grew in the context of your goal (your story arc)
3 Five strengths that helped you achieve success in your goal

Let's looks at examples from our three Hollywood movie icons to see how this works.

Erin Brockovich
1 Starting point: At the beginning of the film, Erin is a mother of three, jobless, and a car accident victim—she's an underdog
2 Arc: From broke and jobless to a millionaire legal advocate
3 Strengths: Smart, resourceful, hard worker, determined, passion for justice

Jason Bourne
1 Starting point: At the beginning of *The Bourne Identity*, Jason is an amnesiac, a gunshot wound survivor, and also an underdog
2 Arc: From amnesiac to self-actualized
3 Strengths: Fit, determined, smart, polyglot who can kill someone with a paper clip, resourceful

Akeelah Anderson

1. Starting point: At the beginning of *Akeelah and the Bee*, Akeelah is bullied for being smart, and she lacks confidence and is socially awkward
2. Arc: From unsure of herself to confident
3. Strengths: Smart, hard worker, coachable, loyal friend, good heart

20-20 Hindsight

Sometimes, you will have a clearer perspective of your starting point once your story is over and you have gained some distance from it. Many people are uncomfortable listing their strengths—or they have blind spots in doing so. But hindsight can provide some surprising revelations. That's the value of analyzing your success trilogy and choosing stories from ten or twenty years ago rather than from last month or last year.

Francesca, a master class student and cofounder of an East Coast-based cannabis company, got stuck thinking about why she *couldn't* accomplish her current goal instead of why she *could*. "My excuses and insecurities came to the surface easier than anything else. I am uncomfortable listing strengths," she said. She found it a lot easier to identify five strengths from her past successes. The DNA analysis of her first story looked like this:

Controlling the Story

1. Starting point: Before she went into marketing, she began her career as an idealistic young teacher, but she was quickly hit with the realities of the education system that made her feel worthless

Recalling, rediscovering, and otherwise identifying your strengths is the first step to leveraging them.

2 Arc: From stuck to finally leaving her job to fulfill herself professionally, and to begin a new chapter to find out who she was and what she was capable of

3 Strengths: Stubborn/committed, tenacious/fighter, strong desire to understand self, empathic, idealistic

In her second story, Francesca was frustrated and tired of the curriculum as she prepped for another school year with books and courses that were decades old. She noted her strengths: driven, passionate about pushing against the status quo, lover of literature, creative, desire to serve students. Her third story was more personal, as it was about the death of her formerly conjoined twin, and how she moved from shock, grief, and fear to peace and gratitude. She identified her strengths in this story as unique relationship and love, the strength to shoulder emotional load, being tapped into feelings, being a good writer, and emotional strength.

Francesca's goal in the master class was to author a definitive cornerstone book that would help others free themselves from the limitations that come up from unhelpful stories they tell themselves. Ultimately, she listed these strengths that would propel her forward in her pursuit: tenacious, creative, decent writer, desire to serve a higher calling, good communicator.

I've seen a range of responses to this exercise, from struggle to exhilaration. It can sometimes seem easier to default to "I can't" or "I don't know" in a recent story, so to bypass your neural circuitry, go deeper into your past, where it's often easier and more comfortable to look at situations with a bit of distance. Take stock and consider where you are as you contemplate where you want to go.

Your job with this work is to start carving from a proverbial slab of marble. Nothing is meant to be perfect on the first try. It is all a work in progress and should be treated as such. Play with it. Take that hunk of clay or marble and work from there. You will get it. Changes and recognition of nuances are part of the process and to be expected. Those who can accept and allow that will have the most fun and success with this work.

If You Get Stuck

If you are really stuck on identifying your uniqueness and fabulousness, ask for help. Here's a sample email to send to three to eight friends and/or colleagues, but only *after* you've done the exercise, please.

> Dear friend/colleague,
>
> I'm doing some life/business/personal/professional analytics to improve my performance, and I'd like to get your perspective on two things, if I may:
>
> 1. What do you see as my strengths?
>
> 2. What do you see as my unique attributes that make me different from others? Or think of the question as filling in this statement: [Your name] is the most _____ person I know. He/she is the best at _____.
>
> Thank you,
> [Your name]

Enchanted by Story

Angeles Arrien was a cultural anthropologist who specialized in transpersonal psychology and the wisdom of Indigenous peoples. Her work was presented at the International Peacemaking Conference alongside three Nobel Prize winners. She won the Benjamin Franklin Award and three honorary doctorates. In her work *Gathering Medicine* (disc 1), Angeles says, "Shaman, medicine men, and healers of many cultures will, across cultures, ask four questions to assess the health and state of a person and community."

Each of Angeles's questions relate to story in some way, but one really stands out: "When did you stop being enchanted by stories, and in particular, your own life story? Stories are globally the greatest healing, teaching art that we have." Angeles also says that we need to remember to acknowledge what is working, because there's more that is working than not.

I say we are living a story. We have choices every single day. Go deep and catalogue your strengths!

EXERCISES

1. Refer to the three success stories you outlined in the previous chapter and complete a character DNA analysis similar to what we did for our film protagonists and Francesca. You can follow this format:

   [Name of Story]
   1. Starting point: _____ (Who are you and how do you show up in your story?)
   2. Arc: _____ (Where did you start and where did you end?)
   3. Strengths: _____ , _____ , _____ , _____ , _____

   (Create an inventory of at least five positive personal strengths for each of your three success stories. There can be an overlap of the same strengths, so don't worry about repeats.)

2. Reviewing the strengths from each of your three stories, write down five positive personal attributes that will help you achieve your current goal.

3. Observe (versus judge) what comes up for you as you do this. Is it easy, matter-of-fact, difficult, a reach to get to five each time, expanding, exhilarating? Do you feel doubt, joy, reassurance, uncertainty? Note your experience. If there is a pattern, you can use The Hollywood Approach to manage these patterns later.

4   Write down a minimum of three key insights or observations from the first part of your character DNA exercises. This can be anything that stands out to you as new, remarkable, interesting, or otherwise noteworthy.

Knowing your own strengths is a critical exercise to your success map. You are the hero or heroine of your story.

CHARACTER DNA PART II: AMNESIA AND SUPERPOWERS

• • • • •

"A peacock who rests on its feathers is just another turkey."

DOLLY PARTON

IN A QUIET moment in a European truck stop, Jason Bourne reveals to his wing-woman, Marie Kreutz, that he knows how much cash is in the till, where the owner hides his gun, and the location of all the exits. He doesn't exactly know how he knows these things, but he is certain that they are true. The context of his situation: Jason is feeling pressure to keep moving, a responsibility to keep Marie safe, and is compelled to find his identity, all of which may trigger these special skills to come to the forefront. His highly specialized skill set functions as a superpower that helps him achieve his goal.

In the context of the movie world, "amnesia" and "hidden superpowers" are linked to the main character's goal, thus fueling the story. And that's how I want to encourage you to view them here. As we go through life, we *all* have forgotten skills, underutilized talents, and untapped gifts. Once-impassioned interests fall by the wayside when we move on to a new chapter—when we change course, we may shift to using different assets and strengths, leaving others behind. Later, we can activate or reactivate these strengths, creating a vantage point from which to work on our current goal.

Don't be mistaken: this is not about bringing out your inner Jason Bourne. This is about bringing out your inner *you*.

Strength versus Superpower

You may wonder what the difference is between a strength and a superpower. Think of it this way: strengths are things we are good at, that we're above average at, things we may share with others and that may be more general:

- She's a great driver in bad weather.
- She has an ear for languages.
- She makes the best chocolate cake.

A superpower is like an up-leveled strength. It's an exceptional or extraordinary ability. In the context of a film, a heroine's relevant superpower is the one that specifically contributes to her overcoming the obstacles to achieving her goal. Think of it this way:

- She is an expert at driving in blizzards and hurricanes because of her extreme ability to focus and tune out all else.
- She can speak a new language in as little as three days.
- Her chocolate cake can incite world peace.

If you're reading the above examples and thinking they're beyond the level of any skill you have, hold tight. You could be in a state of amnesia, and I promise if you dig deeper and consider the framing of your skills, you'll get to your superpowers, too. For example, I have an insanely heightened sense of smell. I could be a character on a CSI show except that this superpower is completely non-cinematic. For years, I have bemoaned it, because I can smell cigarette smoke and usually other foul odors from a full mile away.

Joy Milne, a retired nurse from Edinburgh and a "super-smeller" like me, had noticed that her late husband had a distinct odor. She picked up the same scent when they went to an event with a group of Parkinson's patients. This led to the scientific confirmation that people with Parkinson's disease have a distinct odor—the one that Joy identified. More importantly, according to a BBC story, the odor is present long before physical symptoms of the disease appear. In order to mimic what we can do naturally, science has to use a mass spectrometer.

So please, no matter how far-out or unglamorous your ability might seem, don't negate your mad skills. You just might be waiting for the situation and context in which they can shine. For Kendra, that came in an unexpected way.

La Jefa

"Fire everybody," Kendra's boss told her.

"What?" she said. "I've got only forty-five people in dealer school right now." Was this a joke?

"The whole floor. All the dealers. Make it happen," the owner said.

Casinos have winning streaks and losing streaks—just like customers. As is common in the industry, this owner was superstitious. He also believed the dealers were in cahoots with the customers and one another. Stealing and distrust are the two hallmarks of the business. It's just how it is.

Prior to Kendra's arrival for the casino job in Santo Domingo in 1982, the pit bosses and floor bosses did whatever they wanted. Nobody checked what they were doing with any of the millions of dollars in daily revenues from the fifteen poker tables, ten blackjack tables, and eight roulette tables. So Kendra's arrival meant, for them, an almost certain loss of freedoms.

For Kendra, the casino job in the Caribbean had sounded glamorous. An adventure to be accepted. After all, she'd have a swank penthouse residence, designer clothing, and a private chef. This Catholic New Englander had no idea what she was in for. Learning fluent Spanish in less than a year so she could talk to the four hundred mostly male employees was just the beginning. She was hissed at, followed, and undermined every step of the way.

Two decades after President Trujillo's dictatorship ended, the country's work culture was still highly misogynist and macho. At that time, the Dominican Republic was only beginning its transition to democracy. The very existence of a woman with a job was perceived as a stab in both eyes to the average male. On top of that, she was a gringa and a boss. Or "gringa bitch," as they called her—the least offensive of the atrocious, aggressive behavior she endured. The fact that she went from food and beverage manager to casino manager in a year didn't improve her popularity. Now she had to fire most of the staff.

So she called everybody into the auditorium and announced the dismissals.

"You're not fucking doing this," one male employee said. A mob of echoes followed.

But she was. And she did. Surrounded by security guards, she handed the newly fired employees cash for their severance. With that, she cut a main artery of the power structure of the casino's old guard.

This event marked a turning point. The employees realized that she had authority. Still, it was not easy. It was anything but easy. And she had to rebuild.

The first step was to set up new staff. This meant she had to cut down the hours and the number of tables at first because there was no one to staff them. She went around town and recruited dealers from every casino she could—also not a popular move. The employees realized she was calling the shots. Making the decisions. Doing the hiring. She was really running things. She was no longer an outsider; she had become one of them, in a way. Her superpower was her athlete's mindset—getting the ball across the finish line regardless of who's trying to take you down.

And sure enough, the winning began. With that, a new moniker for her emerged: *La Jefa*, "the Boss." Kendra's fight to prove herself in this colossal uphill battle was over.

"What has stayed with me has empowered me," Kendra said. "Because once you do something like that, whatever your story is, whatever you're doing, whatever you do to overcome situations, the strength, I think, does stay inside you."

Discovering Your Superpower

You may discover that one or more of your strengths are superpowers. In the context of being your own hero, your superpowers are perhaps more unique, more distinctive, and maybe something only you can do—or only you do in your special way or in a particular group or setting. Perhaps, like Jason Bourne's or Joy Milne's, your superpower is revealed only in specific or unusual circumstances. This is exactly why it's so important to go back and mine the gold from your own success stories—to "wax on, wax off" in your story forensics—to uncover hidden personal assets that you may have forgotten about.

No one can shine your kind of bright or live your exact story except for you. No one but you knows the volume of sheer will you used to arrive at this precise point on your path, to not give up when it felt as if all were lost, to speak up at a critical moment when no one wanted to hear from you. No one but you knows what it took for you to take the big leap, the single step that changed the course of your life, to move onward and upward in a crucial moment.

Only you understand the nuances of what will make you take the leap or walk away, whether you are driven by sheer will or a connection to something else. Only you know what really and truly, deep down in your soul, makes you tick when that moment of truth arrives. Your specific perspective, life experience, special knowledge, and skills training—the stuff that enables you to live and *advance* your story in your unique way—is all you. And as the screenwriter of your life, you need to tap into this. So while it is fun to put it in the context of amnesia and superpowers, calling forth your inner hero is critical work.

That said, let's go further into the concept of amnesia and superpowers. The amnesia part is a call to action for you to go back, to dig deeper into the recesses of your mind and your life to rediscover your DNA.

Go after the good stuff—the magical stuff—that may have been forgotten, hidden, or suppressed for any variety of reasons. This stuff could be things that were obvious in one context and time but aren't now, or it could be something literally right in front of your eyes, hidden in plain sight, as it was for Katherine Johnson, who worked at NASA, portrayed in *Hidden Figures*.

Iconic Reinforcements

Whatever your situation, you can find reinforcements within yourself. Let's look at our film examples for more inspiration.

> "Every time we have a chance to get ahead, they move the finish line."
>
> MARY JACKSON
>
> ---
>
> Katherine Johnson and her colleagues Dorothy Vaughan and Mary Jackson crossed all gender, race, and professional lines with their brilliance and extraordinary abilities. The three women were the brains behind one of the greatest operations in US history: putting the first person in space.
>
> *Hidden Figures* is a 2016 biographical drama starring Taraji P. Henson as NASA employee Katherine Johnson, an analytic geometry specialist; Octavia Spencer as acting supervisor Dorothy Vaughan; and Janelle Monáe as aspiring engineer Mary Jackson. The film chronicles the struggles in the 1960s workplace and how the women's exceptional intelligence and mathematics skills enabled them to overcome debilitating gender and race inequities and put the first person in space. You may not have a way of knowing today what flexing your superpower could mean for the person after you, or how it may shape the next generation. What's important is that you do your best in this moment.

Erin Brockovich, Commanding a Job from Ed Masry

This one may very well be my favorite example of any Hollywood character demonstrating any lesson.

Our dear Erin Brockovich.

After the opening scene of Erin's failed job interview, having lost her court case, several of her calls to attorney Ed Masry go

If you want the thing
that stirs your soul,
you're in the right place.

unreturned. Ed arrives at work one day to find Erin in his office, not just waiting for him but working. His secretary whispers, "She thinks she's working here." When Ed questions Erin (my favorite part), she tells him he obviously needs help because no one in his office can return a damn phone call. He rebuffs, saying that's not how things work. She tells him in a low tone to try her for a week, and that he can fire her if it doesn't work out.

Erin works hard, is ballsy, doesn't take no for an answer, and negotiates every point brilliantly. If that's not a lawyer, I don't know what is. And whether or not you want to call that attribute something she had amnesia about, a secret superpower, or an untapped skill, it leads her to her destiny. The real-life Erin Brockovich is still an advocate today. If you're not following her, see what she is doing to continue advocating for water safety. She's magnificent.

Jason Bourne, the Park Scene

Jason Bourne, rescued at sea and befriended by a group of fishermen, eventually recovers enough from his injuries to start investigating the chip implanted in his hip and the mysterious bank account number. He leaves the boat with little cash, wearing his orange sweater with a bullet hole, and camps out on a park bench while he waits for his next mode of transportation to be available the following morning. Awakened by two security guards, Bourne attacks. In that moment, he first realizes he is capable of some super-badass moves.

Akeelah Anderson

Akeelah's love of words is her extraordinary attribute—her superpower. She has a penchant for memorizing and can practice tirelessly for hours on end. She is also connected to words and spelling through her memory of her close relationship with her father, before he passed. She further boosts her strong memory by jumping rope as a mnemonic device for counting syllables in words.

Her story is a call for us to consider our own journey and ask better questions. Which allies can you align with to acquire knowledge and information faster? What qualities and tools do you have that you are not acknowledging or using enough? Consider how they might influence the speed and tone of your journey if you could tap into these aspects of yourself.

The Long Haul

Like Erin Brockovich, you are magnificent, too, and The Hollywood Approach is all about putting together the components that bring out the best in you. Does Erin make mistakes? Yes. Will you? Yes. The idea of perfection is a fleeting, unattainable concept, a constantly moving target. It's crazy-making and a poor choice for focus, because it simply doesn't exist. But your superpowers do.

In my master class, Brian, an Atlanta-based attorney, wanted to take the plunge into the creative realm and start a TV program. He did a deep dive for his superpowers and identified grit, seeking professional advice, and getting comfortable with increasing levels of risk. He said, "A huge part of my hang-up is that I have no idea what I'm doing. I want big results. This is, no doubt, a long road, and it will require a lot of grit, and I need to be prepared for that." This is a universal truth for anyone pursuing their next wildest dream.

After considering how his goal would look when applying his superpowers, Brian realized that his journey "will move faster and mistakes will be quickly dealt with and more easily overcome." He said, "When I activate these superpowers toward my current goal, it will be so damn fun. I know myself, and when I truly bring my best self to the work I'm doing, there is just no stopping me."

Art Is Messy, and So Is Life

If you can do one thing for yourself while you read this book, please do this: practice the concept of acceptance. Accept the idea that the artistic interpretation of your life is a constant work in progress. Things aren't going to fit into neat little boxes. Life will get messy along the way. Figure out how to roll with that and you will be ten—if not a hundred—steps ahead of the game. Why? Because you will streamline the precious time that many people spend deliberating, procrastinating, and perfecting things that can never be perfect.

What you can do is move. You can try. You can be on your path. You can accept who and where you are. There is a journey, effort, lessons, falling down, and getting back up again. Your learning and growth and arc—your transformation—comes from getting in the game and playing full-out. Show up in your story, in this show you call life. Tap into every facet of who you are and all that you have to give, and be the best—the very best—you can be. That is Brockovich-style magnificence. And we are all capable of it.

Keep in mind what Erin, Jason, and Akeelah have in common: they have everything they need already within them. And so do you. Call forth what is already within you. Shake it up a little, maybe add an ice cube or two, and give it a new spin.

Storytelling Is Cranial Pinball

Neuroscience studies show that we have the potential to experience a profound connection when engaging in a story versus just words or data. If, instead of reviewing feature film examples and your own personal stories, you simply read a list of tasks, you would engage two areas of your brain: Broca's area, which handles language processing, and Wernicke's area, which deals with language comprehension.

Consuming and engaging in stories, however, activates Broca's and Wernicke's areas of your brain, plus five more—your visual cortex, olfactory cortex, auditory cortex, sensory cortex, and cerebellum. Storytelling is like an amazing game of cranial pinball. Studies have shown that engaging in stories lights up your brain and fires up oxytocin and dopamine—pleasure endorphins—in your system. This includes stories about yourself. So go deep into your past success stories as you plot your future successes. The way is within you, and reviewing your past successes in detail, exploring themes and aspects of them, encourages your neural pathways in the right direction—forward.

EXERCISES

1   Identify one superpower for each of your success stories. This could also be a new look at the strengths you've already identified to see how potent they really are. Think of traits, skills, or talents that are underused, underappreciated, under wraps, or otherwise secret or forgotten.

2   Imagine that you reclaimed these skills. Write about how these superpowers could help you achieve your current goal. Journal and/or talk this through with a partner.

3   If you activated your superpower(s) toward your current goal, what would be possible for you? Would your journey or success picture be different? Easier? More fun?

4   Next, let's go deeper with a superpower inventory. Get a piece of paper and do a quick journaling sprint. I'll prompt you with a series of questions to trigger memories and stories that you may have forgotten. And... go.

- What did you do as a fifth grader when you lost track of time?

- What did you learn about yourself the first time you made a big move away from home?

- What were you best at in your first job? What did you love about it?

- What would people be surprised to know about you?

- Think of old friends and different times of your life to explore this topic, like in kindergarten, grade school, high school, university, different jobs, vacation time versus work time, weekends versus week days... what did you do in your free time?

Answer the following questions, rapid-fire style. Write down or say out loud the first word that comes to you. The idea is to trigger information in the form of memories and stories that you can mine for clues about your amnesia and superpowers.

- What sports, music, arts, or other activities did you do in school that you no longer do?
- What was your first car?
- Where did you speak your first foreign language outside your home country?
- What was the first new town, city, state you visited?
- What about the first new country?

5 List five insights, observations, or lessons learned from the work you did in this exercise.

CHARACTER DNA PART III: FLAWESOMENESS

· · · · ·

"I finally realized that owning
up to your vulnerabilities
is a form of strength."

LIZZO

In the first few minutes of meeting Erin Brockovich on film, we learn that she smokes, dresses inappropriately for a job interview in health care, talks too much, overshares about her personal life, and has no professional work history. But as the film carries on, we also see that Erin is smart, resourceful, a hard worker, has a fierce sense of what's right and wrong, and has an unwavering commitment to a better life for her kids. Also, she wins an unprecedented case with six hundred plaintiffs against utility giant PG&E for a record $333 million settlement, the largest of its kind in the United States. So there's that.

You cannot look at only the flaws of a character—or of yourself as the hero of your own story—any more than you can avoid your strengths or superpowers. To create a masterpiece, you must analyze the whole picture so that you capture all the depth, all the wonderful parts, and your full dimension as a human being.

Flawesomeness is a highly scientific calculation involving your *flaws* and *weaknesses* plus your *awesomeness*. Flaws are calls to action. Calls to embrace what is—to accept it. Sometimes, they are calls to appreciate or take on a new perspective. This is not scolding our inner or outer child, but rather grown-up self-reflection that fuels real-life capabilities and action planning.

Bottom line: to be your own heroine, you have to address your flaws.

Admitting to, accepting, or—especially—embracing your flaws and weaknesses is not always easy. But if you're going to script a life like the hero you're meant to be, you need to tackle this next.

The awareness and acceptance of your flaws and weaknesses will enable you to develop strategies to mitigate, minimize, or overcome these attributes. It might seem kind of scary at first, but I urge you stay with this, especially within the context of your goal. Don't look away. Don't gloss over possibilities. Don't circumnavigate or otherwise resist or avoid this lesson. The truth is, these aspects of our personality and being are what make us interesting, dimensional, and unique.

There is power, strength, and leverage to be found in being acquainted with our flaws and weaknesses. Only by giving them air, light, and space can we glean valuable information that can make our path toward our goal that much faster, easier, and way more fun. You are *ready* for this. And you might be surprised... about what surprises you.

The first step to addressing flaws is getting your perspective in check. If we are willing to acknowledge that every perceived flaw can also be a strength in the right situation, why, then, are we so intolerant of real and perceived flaws? Many cultures hold up the ideal of perfectionism as the gold standard:

- Got a dent in your car? Bring it to the body shop.

- Picked up a box of crackers at the grocery store that's smooshed? Replace it for a pristine one.

- Got a pimple or a mole? Use a zit cream, bleaching agent, ten layers of concealers, powders, and other cover-ups, pronto.

Perfectionism Is a Fallacy

Perfectionism is the imaginary friend of your adult life. Don't fall for it. Consider how much money Americans alone spent on elective plastic surgeries in 2015. In the United States, we are so averse to our perceived physical flaws that we chose to spend $15 billion correcting them, according to Reuters. *Fifteen billion dollars*. That means, on average, one out of sixteen people spent $7,500 on plastic surgery. A Norwegian study shows that after a plastic surgery, people are more likely to suffer depression, alcoholism, and other disorders.

Scooch over in the cockpit, so I can skywrite this please: Covering up our flaws doesn't work.

And yes! It can be awkward, uncomfortable—even painful—to have flaws. It's not easy. But that's not the only reason we cover up our flaws.

The problem is, in the show we call life, other people are writing our script. Companies and other entities have concocted solutions to flaws and problems we didn't even know we had. And they tell stories about them so we buy into it all. Food, fashion, pharmaceuticals, medicine, and, yes, plastic surgery. These companies and their elaborate marketing and communication strategies are interlopers in our subconscious. In the United States and other parts of the world, we have subscribed to a story of speed, convenience, and perfection being the ideal. But is that what we *really* want? Or is this a finely crafted illusion, a story written by someone else for the sake of profit, that we've bought into? Big-picture thinking, carving a new path, and writing your own script aren't usually convenient.

Those who do story well—like fast food joints and "frankenfood" manufacturers and pharmaceutical companies—reap these benefits of influencing you. Knowing that our subconscious mind works a thousand times faster than our conscious mind, we need to be aware that some of the stories influencing us are designed for someone else's agenda.

Wabi-sabi and Kintsugi

Wabi-sabi is a concept in traditional Japanese aesthetics. It's based on the world view of the acceptance of imperfection. This concept celebrates beauty that is imperfect, impermanent, and incomplete. Characteristics of wabi-sabi include asymmetry, roughness, simplicity, and appreciation of natural objects and processes. Wabi-sabi means "to find beauty in broken things or old things."

Wabi-sabi is also often combined with the Japanese practice of kintsugi, an art form used in pottery to fill the holes of cracked or chipped pieces with gold. While the Western view of broken objects is that their value is decreased, kintsugi followers believe that never-ending consumerism is *not* spiritually rewarding. They follow a philosophy not of replacement, but of awe, reverence, and restoration. The gold-filled cracks of a once-broken item are a testament to its history. Japanese artist Muneaki Shimode says that the "importance in kintsugi is not the physical appearance, it is... the beauty and the importance [that] stays in the one who is looking at the dish."

What if we applied the philosophies of wabi-sabi and kintsugi to the story of our life? Let's look at our imperfections and flaws as interesting, a sign of life—real life—something that's spiritual, connective, enlightening. Let's accept them, revere them, and fill our imperfections—and each other's imperfections—with gold. Let's rewrite our stories for more acceptance, more authenticity, more collaboration, more connectedness. We are all writing our way through plot twists, flaws, and obstacles to get to our goals. We can fill in our flaws with gold.

You'd Do It with Your House

Say you're in the market for a new house, and you find a fixer-upper for $250,000. It has structural issues, chips in the walls and doors, a weird doorway that you don't like. Plus, it needs new paint. What would you do? Hire an architect to protect your investment and get some plans made to do this right. Right?

Why, then, would you not do this for your life? You would, you should, you can! Just as a Hollywood screenwriter does it for an action hero, you can do it for your life. And whether you do it consciously or unconsciously, or you go back and forth, make no mistake: you are the screenwriter of your show.

A heads-up, dear friend: this is not a job interview. The purpose of this exercise is to do the opposite of what you were trained to do in that situation, which is to list weaknesses that are not so secretly also strengths, such as, "I have a habit of over-committing," or, "I'm a workaholic." This work is just for you. You will get the most out of it if you truly identify your honest-to-goodness flaws and weaknesses. Of course, some of your flaws and weaknesses *will* turn out to be advantageous as you make an action plan for your goal. But start by being as honest and as forthright as you can when evaluating yourself.

> "When you're hiding, you're safe, because people can't see you. But funny thing about hiding, you're even hidden from yourself."
>
> YOUNG JOY TO JOY DURING A DREAM
>
> ---
>
> Joy Mangano is a struggling airline agent with a complicated family life who designs and builds an innovative self-wringing mop. She uses her gumption to get on QVC, pitch her product, and change the entire trajectory of her life. The biographical film *Joy* was released in 2015, starring Jennifer Lawrence as Joy, who shows us how it's possible to blow past our flaws and weaknesses by leveraging our strengths, allies, and focus, and by believing in ourselves and taking chances.
>
> Hiding does not truly keep you safe. To be who you are meant to be, you must step up and step out, and show yourself and the world what you can do.

Keeping It Real

In the spirit of keeping it real, I'll share the following story.

I had two fatal flaws in my pursuit of overcoming panic attacks in the water. That's why it took me ten years to do it. First, I refused to believe I was having panic attacks. You can call it a lack of clarity or inability to accept, or just plain being a dum-dum. In my defense, it was an extremely incredulous proposition. Up until the panic attacks, all forms of water—pools, lakes, oceans, waterfalls, and even soaking tubs—had been my happy place. Which leads me to fatal flaw number two. As a result of my disbelief, to prove I wasn't having panic attacks, I performed increasingly risky stunts, the worst of which was "roping" in Lake Michigan. This is hands-down the absolute dumbest thing I've ever done in my entire life. For the uninitiated, roping is jumping off the back end of a moving speedboat, rope in hand, and getting pulled behind the boat. I was told that wearing a lifejacket would make the experience like waterboarding because of the way the water flows through the jacket. So I didn't wear one. It turns out it was like waterboarding anyway. This "stunt," if you can call it that, ended with me being practically catatonic. I was unable to move, half-frozen because... Lake Michigan. Three men had to pull me back into the boat because I was unable to climb the ladder. This, ladies and gentlemen, is an example of the power of stubbornness, closed beliefs, and ego. Please, no roping in Chicago. Or anything that resembles it. Ever.

This event also marked a turning point for me. My stubbornness led me to the certainty that I was, indeed, having panic attacks. This was five years after the first one I had, while cliff diving in Capri. And here's the irony. My flaw also served me in the awesomeness of becoming dead set on getting rid of the panic attacks and no one could convince me otherwise—mostly because I didn't tell many people, but that's beside the point.

Hollywood Flawesomeness

Let's turn to our film icons to see how flawesomeness played out in their stories.

Erin Brockovich

We've already talked about some of Erin's flaws:

- Brash
- Not formally educated in law
- Talks too much
- Doesn't wear traditionally professional attire
- Hot temper

In the opening scene, Erin's dressed for brunch, not a job interview, and she talks too much. Throughout the story, we learn that she can also be brash and hot-tempered.

But aren't many of these also strengths? I said that we are *not* playing job interview, but admittedly, some of these flaws and weaknesses do end up fueling advantages and forward movement in our heroes' stories.

Erin's flaws play out as advantages in this context and in this story. She approaches things differently because she's not a lawyer and has no formal legal education, two things that make her more approachable and relatable to the people of Hinkley. While these qualities hinder her in professional settings sometimes, her authenticity and no-nonsense attitude are what enable her to get things done. She thinks outside the box and beelines to direct results because she doesn't have the same concept of limitations as do other people in corporate law firms.

Jason Bourne

Jason has a few flaws to contend with:

- No memory
- He doesn't know what he doesn't know
- No friends or family

- Debilitating flashbacks
- Has a tendency to meticulously plan things, avoiding simple solutions
- Assassin

Jason starts out with no memory, so he doesn't even know what he doesn't know. Both are weaknesses to his position. He has no friends or family, no clues that would be a big help to him. His debilitating flashbacks make him scared to know the truth. And when he does find out a little more, he learns that he's an assassin. Probably the biggest flaw or weakness you can have if you know nothing else about yourself.

When Jason finds out he is an assassin, his lack of memory allows him to see that he isn't one at heart, and that he doesn't want to be one anymore. It also clarifies who the antagonist is—the people who run Treadstone.

Akeelah Anderson

I peg Akeelah's flaws and weaknesses as:

- Lack of confidence
- Stubbornness
- Fewer resources than her competitors
- Socially awkward
- Less experience than her competitors

Before she gets to a regional bee, Akeelah is bullied and made fun of for winning a school spelling bee. She is ashamed and embarrassed and returns home, where she has little support. Her spirit is dampened. Perhaps that is part of what makes her such a good friend to Javier.

Akeelah then proceeds to the more advanced spelling bees knowing she's up against tough competition—people with more education and coaching resources than she has. She knows she has to work hard and do so on Dr. Larabee's terms to do her best.

Own Your Flawesomeness

There is no game-changing story or journey without the identification and acknowledgment of your own flaws and weaknesses. Take my master class student Sharon, for example. When she started losing her vision because of complications from childhood diabetes, she wanted to get her financial house in order. Now, we could debate that rather than a flaw, her vision loss was a roadblock over which she had no control or influence, but the point is that it was a personal attribute that could potentially impede her goal.

Sharon felt shame around her failing sight and its ramifications, like not being able to read as much. But in looking realistically at how losing her sight was influencing her ability to reach her goal—and how she could work with it—she realized that building self-confidence would destroy her shame. Sharon said, "The things holding me back from my current goal are completely different (for the most part) from past flaws and weaknesses, so I guess I shouldn't be surprised that this feels new and foreign."

When you are facing any kind of new obstacles, you may also be contending with the phases of grief over abilities or superpowers you no longer have. Similarly, I was in denial about my panic attacks for around five years. Had I been able to accept them sooner, they may not have become so severe. Then again, I wouldn't have arrived at this journey. The point is that acknowledging what's really going on, when you are ready to face it, serves you—even if you're not ready to talk about it out loud, make decisions, take action, or ask for help. Moving forward means identifying and acknowledging your circumstances as they are.

If you feel resistance to identifying your flawesomeness, start simply and small, or even funny. For example, when I started my career at NBC, I couldn't hook up a VCR to save my life. Connecting this large, clunky machine that predated DVRs to your television was the absolute basic of home-related TV tech, and I believed that someone working at a major network affiliate, in this case me, should be able to do at least do that. I mean, how can you work for NBC and know intricate details about elaborate cameras, editing equipment, and set lighting and not know how to connect a VCR cord to a TV and get the image to play? Even though setting up VCRs had nothing to do with my job, I felt as if I should just know this stuff.

My weakness advanced to DVD players, too. The gem in that was that I would put it off, and I moved a lot, so I'd often feel unsettled, as if without my DVD player hooked up, my move-in was incomplete. In addition to not being able to hook up the stuff myself, I also failed to ask for help. So the DVD player would sit there for months on end, maybe till the next move, even. It was a common trend for me, and when I lament about all the lost nights at Blockbuster Video in the '90s that could've been... well, it has made me get over it and arrange for the help I need when I need it. This insight has since crossed over to many areas of life.

EXERCISES

1 Identify five flaws and weaknesses in relation to each of your past stories.

2 Identify five flaws and weaknesses in relation to your current goal. Analyzing your past stories for flaws first allows you some distance, perspective, and acceptance that you won't necessarily get if you jump ahead to the current goal. In some cases, you might also start to see patterns. Many take this exercise in stride, but if you struggle with it and it conjures up negative feelings, try to remember that your core mission is to gather information, not to traverse a black hole of doom. Be gentle and loving with yourself. Look at yourself with accepting eyes, the way your best friend would.

3 When you've completed the above two tasks, record three key insights or lessons about how you felt or what you learned about yourself in this exercise.

Then get on with it like the heroine or hero you are. Information is power and you are mastering it.

ALLIES: THE FORCE MULTIPLIER

• • • • •

"If I have someone who believes
in me, I can move mountains."

DIANA ROSS

After my cousin's wedding and a couple of days into my trip to the Dominican Republic's North Coast, I came to the difficult realization that I wasn't going to be jumping into 27 Waterfalls anytime soon. I had been overzealous in my forecast of doing the deed inside of a week. I held firm (flawesomeness: stubborn) on being willing to risk cardiac arrest; I just didn't want to take that risk so soon. Panic still swelled every time I got into the pool or ocean. No way was I going to be ready in a week.

I was in a small town. I spoke Spanish, emphasis on the "ish," and I didn't know a soul. I was staying in a one-bedroom, uninspiring apartment feeling lost and defeated. I had put my luxury hotel clients on pause for this? What was I thinking? I was stuck and had no idea what to do. So I did what any savvy woman in my predicament would do. I went out for brunch.

Just when you think it could not get more poetic than this, it did. I arrived at Friends Café and sat next to two American women who were traveling without intent to go home anytime soon. They were staying in an oceanfront penthouse and invited me to come by for a tour. Oceanfront real estate? Hell, yes! I felt as if I'd hit the jackpot... until we shared stories and they invited me to stay in their guest room. Then I felt like I'd really hit the jackpot... until, a while later, I went swimming with Sheila: the ultimate jackpot.

Let me put it this way: if we could bottle and sell what it's like to stand near or swim with Sheila K. Brown in the ocean, we would be instant gazillionaires. Pure, childlike joy, magic, and awe that is all contagious. Laughter that could cure your deepest heartbreak.

Sheila wasn't the only ally I met on the North Coast in the Dominican Republic. There was also Liz, the vacationing therapist who coached me on managing fear; Maia and Luz, my Danish friends with whom I attempted paddleboarding; and Darrin, who helped me source clothes and navigate technology so I could work while on my improvised, extended stay. Then there were people at karaoke, open mic night, out at the beach, around town. I started to make friends and allies in spades. I was relaxing. Living at the beach. I postponed my flight back to Los Angeles a third time, and that was the final date—I had commitments there. So one week turned into ten, and I was collecting allies almost as fast and on point as Dorothy skipping down the yellow brick road.

Each of them helped me in their own special way with friendship, camaraderie, validation, and support, as well as the mindset and the practicalities of what I was undertaking, not the least of which was getting into the water enough so that the likelihood of cardiac arrest would be less of a risk factor.

Instinctively, I knew I had to have fun. I knew I had to relax and take deadline pressure out of the equation for me to do what I needed to do. Research shows that play impacts the brain by causing the prefrontal cortex to become bigger and faster. This is important because the prefrontal cortex is the brain's executive control center, where emotions are regulated, plans are made, and problems are solved.

Stuart Brown, founder and president of the US National Institute for Play and author of *Play: How It Shapes the Brain, Opens the Imagination, and Invigorates the Soul*, says that emotional control, personal resiliency, and curiosity accrue through developmentally appropriate play experiences. Fun + play = success.

Rally Your Allies

It's easy to underestimate the power of our allies. It's common to miss what's right in front of us. So the big lesson here is: don't be common. In crafting a story for film, Hollywood screenwriters are masters of information, leaving no nugget unused in developing a plot with careful details that get the hero where they want to go.

In part, The Hollywood Approach is a system for managing information. All of our experiences, successes, failures, or pivots are a trove of information from which we can glean important clues to guide us to future successes. Allies—supporters, educators, informers—can come from the most unlikely of places if we are open to them.

When you are pursuing your path to your wildest dream, you will undoubtedly reach a point at which you will have to swallow a tough pill and face something you absolutely do not want to do, then find you don't know what to do, and feel stuck. Applying 100 percent creativity to how you're looking at things, the context you're giving your situation, and how you have the power to change things will shift your entire experience. Your allies can nudge you forward in small and big ways. You never know what small thing can lead to a large new frontier.

Stay open.

An "ally" is a person or entity who supports or encourages you on your path. This can be anyone who makes your journey more informed, supported, comfortable, fun, easy, enjoyable, and successful by any measure. It can be someone who helps you get to the next point or decision, who helps you get or stay in action toward your goal. Allies can be cheerleaders, information conduits, partners. They can be random and serendipitous as well as recruited and planned.

In my completely unscientific estimation, we fail most at this stage: activating our allies. That's partly because we don't recognize that leveraging our allies is a two-way street. We help them, they help us. We help each other get or stay in action, take a break, hit reset, feel useful, find motivation, or connect. Success breeds success. Motivation breeds motivation. Action breeds action. Somebody has to take the first step. It might as well be you.

Amp Up Your Success

As you move into this exercise, think about who your allies are and who they could be. From a story perspective, allies are not necessarily friends, just as antagonists aren't necessarily enemies. They can be, of course, but the definition of allies is a bit broader.

As I mentioned, allies are people and resources that help you—as the heroine—achieve your goal. It's beneficial to identify and be aware of your allies. But when you're pursuing your next wildest dream, knowing who they are is only the first step. Unless you engage and enroll them in your journey, you will be leaving a serious success amplifier on the table. Let's look to our film mentors for some examples.

Allies are your number one secret weapon for acceleration.

Erin Brockovich

Erin's allies are:

- Her children
- Ed Masry
- George
- The Jensens and people of Hinkley
- Charles Embry

Erin's allies are first and foremost her children—Beth, Katie, and Matthew are her love and inspiration. Can allies also be antagonists in the function of the story? Yes. So while young ones inspire and motivate our hero in this story, they also bring complications. We'll discuss those dual and multiple roles in the next chapter. Ed Masry, played by Albert Finney, is the lawyer who, at the beginning of the story, said he could win her car accident case, open and shut. Then he reluctantly agrees to hire her after his firm does not return her phone calls. George, played by Aaron Eckhart, is the neighbor-turned-boyfriend and babysitter. He becomes an ally by agreeing to take care of her kids in the early days of her work on the PG&E case. The Jensens and people of Hinkley are the victims of the lawsuit who, in a story function, become her allies when they agree to proceed with the case, which ultimately leapfrogs her career. Charles Embry is the former employee of PG&E who has documents proving the firm's liability, which he ultimately shares with Erin.

Jason Bourne

Jason's allies are:

- Fishermen
- Marie Kreutz

- Nicolette Parsons
- Marie's ex
- Pamela Landy

In *The Bourne Identity*, Jason picks up allies at critical junctures, and even while unconscious. In the beginning of the story, the fishermen find him floating at sea, unconscious. They bring him aboard their boat, give him food and a place to sleep, and even sew up his wounds. When he's well enough to travel, they give him a bit of money to get started on his journey. He then meets Marie in the embassy. Marie helps him drive to Paris and continues helping him try to recover his memories, as well as keeps him safe. She becomes not only a great ally but also a love interest. Nicolette, Jason's former colleague, helps stall Treadstone while he makes his escape. Marie's ex gives him a place to stay, and Pamela Landy, the CIA department director, wanting to uncover the truth, hears him out. Each ally plays an important role on his path.

Akeelah Anderson

In *Akeelah and the Bee*, Akeelah's allies are:

- Her teachers and Principal Welch
- Dr. Joshua Larabee
- Javier
- Her mother
- Kiana

In *Akeelah and the Bee*, Akeelah has few and precious allies in her pursuit of winning spelling bees. Principal Welch is motivated for her to succeed and arranges private coaching with Dr. Larabee. Her friend Kiana supports her unconditionally.

Akeelah quickly makes friends with fellow speller Javier and attends his birthday party. He also helps show her the ropes around the competitions and introduces her to some of the other competitors. When it comes close to the wire for the national championship, Akeelah makes allies out of anyone and everyone who crosses her path by practicing her words with them—including the mailman, a gangster, restaurant patrons, random people on the street, and even the memory of her late father.

Engaging Your Allies

Once you identify your potential allies, taking action to secure their support is the next key step. Laura Peña, the mastermind behind a project called "She Is the Universe," has interviewed girls aged thirteen to nineteen from six continents. She asked them the same set of questions about their dreams and what they needed to accomplish them. They have various goals: to be writers, artists, scientists, ballerinas. They are all on their path: in lessons, in practice, doing their thing, in flight toward their destinations. When asked what they need to make a difference, forty out of the fifty girls identified the same exact thing: support. They need more help.

Over and over again in my master class, I see that people resist asking for help. They flat-out refuse for different variations of the same reason. They don't want to put someone out; they want to avoid the awkwardness or hurt feelings of a no. One woman, Carole, even said that she feels like she's cheating if she gets help on a goal. It's not uncommon. I feel it myself sometimes. If that sounds like you, you need to shift that mindset, and maybe acquire some tools to help get over the hump. Think through all of the people who would or could benefit from you achieving your next wildest dream. Focus on them. For me, that could literally be anyone in the world who might be stuck in a rip current again when I am around. For Annie, getting fit means longevity: she can stay with her wife and son longer.

Many people in my master classes found that their allies follow them from story to story. Mina, for example, is an entrepreneur who wanted to transition to online sales, but in order to leverage the power of her allies, she had to overcome her tendency to withdraw. Through the allies exercises, Mina was reminded to stay engaged on a regular basis and, in her words, "not be a hermit" to find success. She also realized that she has nothing to lose by consciously recruiting supporters. Mina said, "There are allies around me all the time."

The Art of Asking a Better Question

Help comes in different forms. It can be words of encouragement, a ride somewhere, coaching, manual labor, a witness, a collaborator, a mentor, a critical piece of information or expertise... In considering how to engage your allies, you must first be willing to ask for the help you need. And so, we must talk about the art of asking a better question.

Let's use moving as an example. There is a big difference between asking, "I'm moving. Are you around next Saturday?" and "Would you help me move?" and "Would you help me unpack my kitchen for an hour next Saturday?" The first question is passive and vague. If you want to take a subtler approach, it could work. But your results could vary. The second is direct but still vague. When you make requests, think about them from

> "Even though they're big and powerful, they're so much like us. We're vulnerable. We get scared. And we need help sometimes too."
>
> RACHEL KRAMER
>
> ---
>
> When three majestic gray whales become trapped under five miles of ice in the Arctic Circle, Greenpeace volunteer Rachel Kramer jumps into action to help them. Inspired by actual events, *Big Miracle* is a 2012 film featuring Drew Barrymore as Rachel.
>
> With the clock ticking in Point Barrow, Alaska, Rachel and her ex-beau and newsman, Adam Carlson, rally an unlikely crew of allies, including Inuit, oil companies, the government, media, and Russian and American military, to set aside their differences and carve openings in the ice to free the whales. Also fascinating about this story is the trickle-down effect of goodness—career promotions and personal relationships, including a marriage, that develop as a result of this town and its allies coming together for a common cause. Allies are a force multiplier for you achieving your goal and have the potential to influence others—maybe even everyone—involved in your story.

the recipient's perspective. In order for a friend to assess whether they can help you, they need to know what they're in for. Think of it like a birthday party invitation: who, what, when, why, and where. The third is respectful because you have formed the question after considering what you would like from the person and what their commitment to you is.

What Not to Do

Like many people, I get asked—or not even asked—all the time for help with scripts, screenplays, manuscripts, and speeches. The "request," and I use that term loosely, comes in all kinds of ways. The worst is when people send an unsolicited file with a vague "I'd love to know what you think" or, perhaps the most entitled, no note at all. Even if you are my friend's husband's grocer's dog walker's third cousin, that's presuming a big commitment of up to eight hours of my professional time.

So I am saying seek help from others, but *ask first* and *ask nicely*. Sending unsolicited work of any length is presumptuous and rude. Don't do the equivalent of showing up at someone's home with your dog and expecting them to dog-sit for you indefinitely. That would imply this person is somehow obligated to drop everything to feed and water Fluffy, and clean up his poop. Avoid being that person.

What to Do

The proper way to ask for a favor, especially if you want the results to go in your favor, is to show consideration. Think about the person you're requesting help from. Do a pre-ask.

> Hey, Sallie,
>
> I need some help with my project. I found your previous notes on my work so valuable that I wanted to ask you first. If I outlined a few questions, would you be willing and available to take a look at it in the next two weeks and give me your thoughts on eight questions? It's about a three-hour read. Either way, I greatly appreciate your consideration and look forward to seeing you again soon.

That's a legit request. It's specific, acknowledges the work involved, and gives a clear time frame. An expert ask. Sallie can now evaluate the request and make her decision.

For your story to be a success, you will need to rally your allies. You will have people around you on your path, whether you choose them or not. Why not choose them? People are often so gracious and giving, especially when you share a sense of community. Ask for the help you need.

EXERCISES

1   List five allies who helped you in each of your previous success stories. In addition to people, allies can also be your environment, costumes, venues, markets, world conditions, the place you live in, or yourself. But be specific: What is it about you that makes attracting allies possible? Your drive, your history, your creativity? Your ability to make new friends in five minutes? Here is a prompt for thinking about who your allies were or could be:

- Friends and strangers
- Dream allies
- Wannabe allies
- Mentors
- Role models
- Mindset

2   Identify five allies already helping you reach your current goal.

3 Identify five people who *could* be your allies in pursuit of your goal.

4 Write a sample question or request for help for each of them, using the What to Do and What Not to Do sections as your guide.

5 Record three observations from this exercise.

DRINK YOUR ANTAGONISTS' TEARS

• • • • •

"Life is a ruthless game unless
you play it good and play it right."

TAYLOR SWIFT

"**GO TO HELL.** And do it now." That was the message Pastor James David Manning, of the ATLAH World Missionary Church, aka the "Harlem Hate Church," had for his neighbors at the Ali Forney Center (AFC) for LGBTQ youth experiencing homelessness.

Multiple sources report that Manning had a reputation for regularly flogging hate speech and homophobic slurs using the church and its marquee, podcasts, sermons, online videos, and private family counseling as a medium for this rhetoric. But the church was about be shuttered. Following decades of unpaid water and sewer bills, it had received a statement of foreclosure totaling more than $1 million, according to an MSNBC report.

Down the street, AFC founder Carl Siciliano and local advocates raised $333,000 to try to buy the church at auction and use the property to expand the AFC shelter. However, Pastor Manning went to court for a stay on the foreclosure order and was successful. "The property has been in court ever since. Ultimately, the church will be put back on the auction block," Carl told me.

To categorize Manning as an antagonist to the AFC, its mission, or LGBTQ issues at large is an understatement. Manning's mission of hate and exclusion, reported by numerous media outlets, is the exact opposite of AFC's mission of love and inclusion. "LGBT young people, like all young people, are worthy and deserving of love and respect. I'm proud to have fought to protect and empower these young people who have suffered so much rejection and abandonment over the last eighteen years," Carl told me in an interview.

Ali Forney was a transgender teen who was put out of their home when they were thirteen years old and lived on the streets of New York City for nine years before being murdered at age twenty-two. Their tragic death has never been brought to justice; however, it called attention to the atrocious conditions for homeless LGBTQ youth in New York. Carl, who was named a White House Champion of Change by the then president Obama, committed to honoring Ali's advocacy work by providing health services, life skills, mentorship, and other tools so that the center's clients, who are often in acute crisis, may reclaim their lives and never again live on the streets.

"I'm proud that Ali's life was able to inspire a movement of advocacy among LGBT people in New York that has resulted in such a transformation of what's available for homeless youth," Carl said. He added, "Ali would sometimes sleep in Mount Morris Park, which is at the end of the block where ATLAH is located. It would be very meaningful to me to provide housing for young people a hundred yards from where Ali used to sleep on the streets. Ali was very loving, very supportive and kind, and created a real sense of family and community with the other homeless youth on the streets."

The Necessary Barrier

Action movies illustrate the antagonist's function with crystal clarity: to stop the protagonist from achieving their goal. Nothing inhibits success like blowing up the bridge, stealing the coveted prize, or driving a stake into the hero's heart.

But even when the worst happens, when all is lost and it's the dark night of the soul—when it *feels* like the main character will never, ever recover—you know the sun will shine again, a new act will commence, and figuratively and literally, the protagonist will turn the page and start a new chapter. This is usually a moment when all the forces around the character—her weaknesses, flaws, and antagonists—come out of the woodwork at once to overpower the heroine in a negative way, to bring us to the worst possible moment.

No amount of evil, fiction or nonfiction, is a match for us. Why? Because good overpowers evil and love is stronger than hate—and science proves it. More to come on that. So when it comes time to think about derailing your antagonists, you need to do two things. First, you need to identify the internal and external antagonists on the path to your current goal. Then, you need to activate strategies to neutralize them.

Hollywood Antagonists

Our three go-to archetypes can show us examples of internal and external antagonistic forces.

Erin Brockovich's Antagonists

Erin's antagonists included her personal weaknesses, as well as the Goliath that is PG&E and PG&E's counsel:

The thing about antagonists in real life is that they are usually no match for our sheer will to create our happy ending.

- Herself
- PG&E
- Ed Masry (at first and when he partnered with another firm; but he is also an ally)
- Charles Embry (the scary guy who seemed like trouble but was actually a major ally)
- PG&E's counsel

In Erin's view, and understandably, she saw many people as antagonistic forces. When we're pursuing a better life, antagonists and even we ourselves can also be allies. Even though creating a better life for her children was Erin's goal, her kids also sometimes hindered her progress in doing her job—which was a part of reaching that goal. They required time, attention, love, and care, and that was an opposing force in her objective.

Jason Bourne's Antagonists

Although he had many allies, Jason Bourne also faced multiple antagonists:

- The police in the park, early on
- Police and security at the embassy
- The CIA's black op Treadstone
- The professor, who tried to kill him

Jason had trouble with not only his memory but also authority. Starting with the police in the park, and soon after, the security at the embassy, Jason faced off with people trying to move him off his mission. This revealed some of his strengths—his fight skills and logistics. Treadstone tried to kill him. You can't get more antagonistic than an assassin. The CIA's motivation was to cover up their screwup with the program. Not cool. And JB was not having it.

Akeelah Anderson's Antagonists

As with Erin's list, you'll notice some crossover between Akeelah's allies and antagonists:

- Her mother
- Bullies at school
- Javier
- Devon
- Kiana

In *Akeelah and the Bee*, Akeelah faces a unique situation in which her competitor turns into her ally and friend. Devon, who is cold, withdrawn, and reserved, makes it to the end of the bee with Akeelah, changing the entire dynamic of their relationship, interaction, and the competition itself. Together, because of their hard work and serious effort, they raise the game and inspire all who know them.

Your Own Worst Enemy

In real life, your antagonistic forces are not as obvious as a vampire wearing all black, darting among Gothic architecture as he trails you through an overcast, evocative location while you're wearing the same ripped-up clothes for three days in a row. Hopefully, antagonists like the Harlem Hate Church are few and far between—but they do exist. In real life, our antagonist forces are often ourselves. They are the things we do and think that not only slow us down but also have the ability to stop our show. They could be a flaw or weakness on steroids.

The antagonistic forces that are of the personal and internal variety often show up in real life as indecision, fear, doubt, discomfort, uncertainty, indecisiveness, unwillingness to take action, and so on. They are examples of *you* stopping you.

Meredith, from my master class, who was rebranding her business to be in alignment with her authentic inner self, said, "I see myself as the biggest antagonist. Mindset plays a role, though I am aware of the limiting beliefs that typically get in the way, and I'm working on them." Interestingly, Meredith consistently identified her strengths as courage and resourcefulness in her three past success stories. This irony and a push-pull of "good versus evil" is within many of us when we are facing down our antagonists.

Volumes have been written on the subject of managing fear and doubt. From the screenwriter's perspective, when cramming the story into less than two hours, the strategy is simple: heroes feel the fear and do it anyway. In the film world, story elements are crafted around a "dark night of the soul" moment to create a satisfying experience for the audience. The hero must make a leap, and a big one, otherwise... you know... it's not a movie. Or it's a sad and disappointing movie in which the hero doesn't obtain his goal.

You'll experience such moments in real life, too, when your flaws seem to be on steroids and threaten to stop your show. That's when you have to summon your will and choose a mindset of courage to take that leap. As another master class student, Megan, put it, "I know that I need to keep working on my mindset to get back to a place where I have more confidence in my actions, knowing that failure is a possibility but that, without taking the risk, I will have no gains."

When an Antagonist Is an Ally

External antagonists don't necessarily have evil intentions, although it may feel like they do. They're whomever or whatever has a goal in direct opposition to yours. External antagonists may be a family member, colleague, friend, enemy, frenemy, competitor, boss, loved one, government, evil empire, business.

If your loved ones are hindering your progress in achieving your goal, they are, for structural purposes in this discussion, an antagonistic force, and you need tools and strategies to neutralize that influence and increase your chances of getting to your goal for the greater good. Very often, the main thing that holds us back is the lack of support from the people closest to us. This is why I consider allies the secret sauce. You must seek out allies and community who will support you in the ways you need it most, even and especially if they're super-basic ways, like talking, listening, and validating. This is also a call to consider from whom and where you might benefit from some distance during your pursuit of this goal so as to lessen the forces working against you.

It's so common to have competing priorities in life, as in the case of Erin Brockovich, who worked hard to up-level her career for her children. Still, in terms of story structure, a sick child is also a force detracting a single mother from doing her work. That is not a comment against children or single mothers—or anyone who needs care or their caregivers. The truth is that we physically cannot be in two places at once—say, at home with our family while at the same time being a field investigator in a major case.

There is a distinct moment before Jason Bourne pulls the trigger in his assassin-to-assassin showdown in the field outside of Marie's ex's house: when he makes the professor his ally and gets more information about Treadstone to help his mission. This calls forth the question in real life: Is there a way to make an antagonist an ally on this specific path? Is it time to metaphorically kill the antagonistic force by disengaging or putting distance between you?

> "I'm not leaving because I'm scared. Or because I think I'm not enough. Maybe for the first time in my life, I *know* I am."
>
> RACHEL CHU
>
> ---
>
> In the 2018 romantic comedy *Crazy Rich Asians*, native New Yorker Rachel Chu, played by Constance Wu, accompanies her boyfriend, Nick Young, to a wedding in Singapore, where she learns his family is extremely wealthy. His disapproving mother, Eleanor, tells Nick he must choose between Rachel and his family. Rachel confronts Eleanor over a game of mah-jongg, stating that she turned down Nick's proposal, and one day, when Nick marries another girl and Eleanor is playing with her grandchildren, it will be because of her, a poor, raised-by-a-single-mother, low-class, immigrant nobody.
>
> Rachel then makes the winning move in mah-jongg and calmly walks away.
>
> To drink your antagonists' tears is to face your antagonists head-on, on your terms, and in a way that leads to a positive result.

How to Drink Your Antagonists' Tears

Good overpowers evil in the same way that love triumphs over fear. But with love and fear, science proves it. Let's talk about the work of Sir David R. Hawkins, MD, PhD, or, as some call him, "Sir Doctor Doctor." Hawkins was a doctor of applied kinesiology as well as a psychiatrist and did extensive work on the power of emotion.

Hawkins's book *Power vs. Force: The Hidden Determinants of Human Behavior* provides scientific analytics on the power of love and fear as well as a wide range of other positive and negative emotions. The Map of Consciousness, also known as the Hawkins scale, measures different emotions from high to low based on millions of calibrations of applied kinesiology tests. For example, positive emotions such as love, joy, and peace calibrate at levels from 500 to 1,000 in a logarithmic progression. Courage calibrates at 200. On the other end of the scale, fear, grief, guilt, and shame calibrate from 100 to 20. Hawkins scale practitioners, in essence, advise that we do not wade into emotions below courage.

This scale is a logarithmic progression, not simply a multiplicative one. So love, at 500, is not just five times more powerful than fear, at 100—it is exponentially more powerful. Love can eradicate fear. By focusing on the good (positive stories and experiences that lead to positive emotions) we can overpower evil (all the negative emotions and narratives such as fear and uncertainty).

If you get stuck any time or place on your journey, try good thoughts and actions. For your own benefit. Love will always override fear and anger. The two cannot coexist. Or do what my dad always said, "Don't get mad, get even." I'd like to add that the framing of that should be coupled with, "Success is the best revenge."

I can't say it any clearer than this: if you are looking at the show you call life from the perspective of a Hollywood screenwriter, and you have identified legitimate antagonistic forces in your story, then someone or some people stand in the way of you reaching your goal. Whether they are a loved one and it is unintentional, or they are a competitor or other person with a different focus, they may delay or derail your plans if you don't take action.

Once you've done the most important step, which is to identify who could scuttle your plans, you've got to figure out what to do about it. You have options to consider and decisions to make. When I'm writing a movie, I see four key opportunities to neutralize antagonists.

1: Consider the Leverage

What else besides stopping you from achieving your goal does the antagonist want? The Brockovich kids wanted some quality time and attention from their mother, something that did not immediately happen during the movie, but she up-leveled her life to give them all a better life. The professor in *The Bourne Identity* wanted to eliminate Jason, but Pamela Landy at the CIA wanted information from him. Jason leveraged that to get what he wanted—information about himself. In *Akeelah and the Bee*, Devon wanted to beat Akeelah in the Scripps National Spelling Bee, yet when she gave him an out, one he knew she knew, he didn't take it and instead raised the stakes and the caliber of the competition for them both with the best possible outcome. Is there any way to align forces with the antagonist? To restructure the relationship? This works especially well if your antagonist is also a loved one.

2: Increase Your Allies

In real life, as well as in film, allies are the biggest secret, yet not-so-secret weapon we all have. If there's one thing to take from this book, it is to be a better ally so that you have better allies. You will need them your whole life through. Who else can you recruit and rally for your cause?

3: Double Down and Recommit to Your Path

For Jason, doubling down and recommitting meant outsmarting the assassin. For Erin, that meant taking a calculated risk to meet the seemingly sketchy guy, to get the document proving PG&E knew of the danger of their actions. Akeelah offered Devon an out, then competed till the very last word. What does doubling down look like for you when the antagonists turn up the heat?

4: Revisit Your Goal Often

Strengthen your mindset and focus on the outcome you want so that all fears, weaknesses, and antagonists fade into the background. When they come back in, you push them back out. It is the theory of light pushing out darkness, hope banishing fear, positive overpowering negative. If something is bringing you down, focus on a better thing. Do not give energy to the negative. Acknowledge it, feel it, deal with it, but aim your focus on your goal.

Carl Siciliano did this consistently with his work and mission to help LGBTQ youth experiencing homelessness in New York, which make up 40 percent of the homeless population. When he first started the Ali Forney Center, he told me that New York sanctioned only about 150 beds for homeless youth. The city now supports 750 beds. Carl's focus on the big-picture goal has had implications beyond the AFC.

What to Do Next

It's eye-on-the-prize time. What to do is jump in, go full out, double down, stare fear in the face, and do what needs to be done. It's you, your goal, and one thing standing between you. It's the moment you decide to go the distance or throw in the towel. It's the moment you decide you want the goal more than the fear wants it, more than the doubt wants it; there's no more time to think it over and decide. It's this one critical moment and it's all on you.

If you've done the exercises I've laid out for you in all of the previous chapters—if you've done the thinking, the plotting, the excavating—you are likely ready for this moment. You know what you're after, you know what you're made of, and you're not going to let anything stop you.

EXERCISES

1   List the external antagonistic forces working in direct opposition of your goal.

2   List the personal (internal) antagonistic forces working in direct opposition of your goal.

3   In what ways are you an antagonistic force in your own game plan? Your mindset? Your actions? The structure of your time or priorities?

4   How could you potentially sabotage your own progress, either subconsciously or with the creep of lingering other priorities or mindset abominations?

5   If you are the biggest antagonist force, take a moment to assess what about you is stopping you. The common ways people play the role of their own antagonist are by not doing enough work on their mindset, a lack of action, the wrong actions, and refusing to ask for help.

6   List three observations that stood out to you from the exercises and lessons in this chapter.

Universal truth: there are fewer actual antagonists in real life than there are in the movies. And I can't say this enough: information is power. Be thorough in this exercise. You will realize hidden or not-so-hidden gems.

MENTORS AND MODELS

"The only way you can sustain a permanent change is to create a new way of thinking, acting, and being."

JENNIFER HUDSON

MENTORS, ROLE MODELS, and coaches play an integral part in our growth, especially when purposely chosen and sought out. In *Akeelah and the Bee*, Dr. Joshua Larabee (played by Laurence Fishburne), a visiting English professor, acts as a quintessential mentor and coach to Akeelah. The story begins with the head of the school, Principal Welch (Curtis Armstrong), asking Akeelah (Keke Palmer) to compete in the Crenshaw Schoolwide Spelling Bee. She initially refuses but has a change of heart under the threat of detention for the rest of the semester.

Akeelah's impressive knack for language and spelling shines as she wins the bee; however, she is shamed and bullied about her smarts. Soon after, Principal Welch arranges a meeting with Dr. Larabee. Still stinging from the bullying, Akeelah is rude to him. She agrees to do the district spelling bee, but Dr. Larabee refuses to work with her. She pulls off a narrow victory—a last-minute hitch when another contestant is caught cheating. This qualifies her to participate in the Scripps National Spelling Bee.

However, based on this experience, Akeelah sees that she is out-resourced and out-experienced, and could be out-maneuvered by her fellow contestants. She needs help and she knows it. She approaches Dr. Larabee and agrees to work with him on his terms. This is where the magic starts happening. Dr. Larabee teaches Akeelah the basis of language: he helps her understand the roots of Latin and Greek words so that she can understand the origin of any word. He gives her the winning words from the past twenty-five national spelling bees to practice with. When he realizes she taps her leg as a mnemonic device, he sees if she can amplify that by jumping rope—which she can. With his guidance, Akeelah's skill and confidence increase even more.

From the beginning of the story, we know that Akeelah desperately misses her father, with whom she shared a love of language and words. So the attention and guidance of Dr. Larabee is very special to her. We learn later that Dr. Larabee lost his young daughter, close to Akeelah's age, to an illness, and that this relationship is special to him as well. They work great together as a team. Akeelah also leans on the memory of her father when she loses confidence or faith in herself; the film shows us examples of a day-to-day coach and mentor, as well as one who is not physically present.

The Bridge between Vision and Action

Iconic characters in our lives, people like Dr. Larabee and Akeelah's father, those who have gone before us and have done what we aspire to do, those whom we admire for their intelligence, patience, and selfless love, can be used as role models and are another way to build a bridge between vision and action, between point A and point B. We know from neuroscience, quantum physics, and modern thinking and practices, how powerful a fully dimensional vision is to achieving one's goal. A survey of the use of visualization was done with US Olympic coaches and

"When the time comes to bet on yourself, I hope you double down."

OPRAH WINFREY

athletes at the Olympic & Paralympic Training Center in Colorado Springs. Ninety percent of the athletes as well as 94 percent of the coaches used imagery in their sport. Ninety-seven percent of the athletes and 100 percent of the coaches surveyed agreed that imagery enhances performance. Many people, including athletes, practice "mental walk-throughs," visualizing their desired outcomes. Imagery primes our mind with electrical transmissions via neural pathways, which signal our senses.

In my journey, and not just the waterfalls one, I often think of my grandmother, Verna Johnson. Grandma's favorite phrase was "give 'er"—she'd use it when playing cards or driving a car or for general purposes. It was fantastic. Also, when I was a kid and she went back to work, she'd send me to the store for treats—a secret we kept from Grandpa. She'd give me $20, nearly a full day's wages after taxes in the early '80s, and ask me to get a Snickers and a Caramello for her, plus whatever I wanted. When I came back with her change, she told me to keep it. I'd protest. She'd say, "Keep the change or I'll never talk to you again." She was baller before "baller" was even a thing. She could've said many other things, of course, like "end of discussion," or "that's final," but her dramatic flair had me at hello. It still makes me laugh to this day.

Another legendary figure I think about often is my parents' neighbor Ruth, in the Upper Peninsula of Michigan. Ruth swam daily in front of their homes, in Lake Gogebic, from May to September. The lake gets to fifty degrees Fahrenheit at best. Ruth would be in there, rain or shine, every day, all summer. She was in her eighties, and she did this every year until she passed away, in her early nineties.

I never met Ruth, but from the stories I've heard, she was an absolute fireball. And when I think it's cold wherever I am swimming, which I can assure you is not in or near Lake Gogebic, I think of Ruth: I visualize her plunging into fifty-degree Lake G—and I get on with it. Not only to swim in the current moment, but to condition myself for the future. Because when I picture myself in my eighties and nineties, I like to imagine myself with a raspy voice doing daring and delicious things, which most definitely includes swimming. Mentors and role models can be tapped in many places.

Your Mount Everest

Climbing Mount Everest. Those are three words that can scare even the best of us. And if you've ever looked into what it really takes to make the climb, it's no wonder it's so often used as a metaphor in the fashion that it is.

First, there's flying into Lukla Airport, which sits on a cliff with a two-mile drop. Some call it the most dangerous airport in the world. All that the pilots (and you) have to do is zip through a tight valley and land on the 0.3-mile runway without going over the edge, Mission Impossible style. From there, you trek for ten days to get to base camp as you start acclimatizing—you know, so the lack of oxygen doesn't take you out. You toughen yourself by doing "up and backs" to and from base camp, increasing your levels of altitude in increments, so your body can make oxygen. Thin air is no joke.

The trip takes an average of eight weeks in a finite window during monsoon season, during which the jet stream and one-hundred-mile-per-hour winds won't blow you off the mountain. Your target for finishing the climb is the last two weeks of May, when the tropical storms form in the Bay of Bengal, move north toward Nepal, and nudge the jet stream off the peak. So if you want up, you have to giddyup right then. And you have to make sure you're on your way, acclimatizing, for the other six weeks so you make it in time.

There's also a spiritual aspect to the climb. In the Himalayas, local Buddhists believe that the mountains are inhabited and controlled by mountain spirits. Most follow an unwritten climbing code, including paying respect to these spirits. So you meet with a lama—a holy person whose role is to draw upon a higher power and ask for the mountain to grant you safe passage. Traditionally, the lama places a necklace on you for protection while on Everest.

Once you're on the ascent, there are other obstacles. Oh, what was that? An icefall? This is a fancy name for a glacial crevasse—which is a fancy name for big hole in the ice cliff you are climbing. As the weather shifts, parts of the ice river melt and refreeze, creating gaps—or crevasses—of around one to three feet wide, leaving a gaping hole where you are supposed to walk. To sum up, you freeze your bum off, the altitude cuts off your oxygen supply, and you face death-defying ice crevasses. Mother Nature has the most dazzling of plot twists.

So do you venture out on a jaunt like this solo? Hell, no! Like Tom, an attorney who attempted Everest in 2018, you get a Sherpa. Tom's Sherpa was Pemba, who grew up in the Himalayas. Pemba is genetically capable of thriving in these conditions and doing a job that very few else can. You also get an icefall doctor—a special Sherpa who sets up ladders across crevasses at the beginning of each Everest season. Icefall doctors return daily to adjust the ladders as the icefall moves. Sometimes, they latch two to three ladders together and stretch them out to cover one of these wide crevasses.

As Tom rightly notes, the concept of the Sherpa applies both to attempting to summit the highest point of the world and to all areas of your life. When you pursue your dreams, you need support from other people; you need a "Sherpa" in all areas of life. Personally, I don't know why anyone in their right mind, or even in their wrong mind, would entertain the idea of climbing the literal or figurative Everest without a Sherpa, guide, lama, coach, icefall doctor, or mentor, and preferably all six, like a backup band. The role is the same: to provide guidance through life's opportunities and tough spots. Why? Because you risk death. Literal death, or the death of your dream.

Sometimes problems require specific mentors, as was true for Tom. He battled spiraling respiratory challenges on his way up the mountain in 2018 and eventually had to be airlifted out. Tom made a second attempt in 2019 with a coach who has summited Everest successfully fourteen times. Again, he did not reach the summit. His guides wanted the other team members to go very fast, at a speed that would help ensure the group's safety, but it was too fast for Tom. He ultimately decided it was best for him to end another trip without reaching his goal. Tom told me in an interview, "The Universe may have been looking out for me. After I came down, an avalanche came down right behind my team. Had I kept going, I would likely have been in the middle of the avalanche because I was moving much more slowly than the team."

Think about the current crevasses in your own life and what kind of approach you are taking to cross them. And as Tom asks, "Who's your Sherpa? Who could help you?" As long as you're not on Everest, there's a good chance your objectives are less risky and more easily navigated than the Khumbu Icefall. But whatever your challenge is, if you're doing it without a metaphorical Sherpa or icefall doctor, consider whether you've architected a path that is the most direct, safest, and best choice for you and the people around you.

The Difference a Mentor Makes

Let's take a look at the kind of difference having a mentor or role model can make.

Michelle Bourdeau had just won first place in the women's division of the 2008 Cabarete Classic, a slalom windsurfing racing event. She was elated, reflecting on her personal-best sailing, as she watched her first-place male counterpart collect his prize: $500. Next, Michelle was presented with her prize: a $40 gift certificate. On the inside, she felt like a volcano exploding. She was outraged.

She decided that she would "right this wrong." Her first instinct was to raise ten times more prize money for the women in next year's competition. But she wasn't completely sold on that idea. Then, a couple of months later, she read about Tatiana Howard, who had had a similar experience on the Professional Windsurfers Association Tour. Michelle decided to leverage Tatiana as a mentor and model. The following year, based on a similar event that Tatiana held in Maui, Michelle hosted the Butterfly Effect: a noncompetitive watersports day open to women in Cabarete.

It's been twelve years since that first event, and in that time, the Butterfly Effect Cabarete has hosted one thousand women participants, removed several tons of garbage from Cabarete beaches, and raised more than $75,000 for The DREAM Project, a nonprofit that provides education to nine thousand children in the Dominican Republic. Most important to Michelle are the women who push past their fear and achieve something on the water that they would never do alone. Michelle told me, "It gives me great excitement, elation, tears, chills, everything—every time I speak about it. It's not just about what we can do, it's about bringing everybody along with us." With Tatiana as a role model and mentor, Michelle left the idea of revenge behind to create an experience that, as she told me, "is so powerful that all the prize money in the world would never make up for it."

Please, find a mentor. Leverage your allies. However crazeballs your situation may seem, support and guidance will be a blessing, and may affect the trajectory of your future.

> **"You have to live the life you were born to live."**
> REVEREND MOTHER
>
> In the 1965 film *The Sound of Music*, Maria is a free-spirited soon-to-be nun who takes a sabbatical as a governess for widower Captain Von Trapp and his seven children and falls in love. Maria must overcome her inner conflict about her destiny and choose the right path for herself. Torn about what to do, she asks for guidance from her mentor, the Reverend Mother, who tells her, "Maria, these walls were not built to shut out problems. You have to face them. You have to live the life you were born to live." Maria decides to marry the captain, and together with the children, they flee across the Alps to safety from the Nazi regime.
>
> Good mentors will nudge you forward on your path, closer to the fullest expression of you, even if your path differs from theirs.

Characters, Mentors

In film, the mentor's role is to provide inspiration, aid, advice, or magical equipment when all appears doomed, to impart a crucial piece of wisdom at a critical juncture in the heroine's pursuit of her goal. Cinderella's fairy godmother tells her to return home by midnight or the stagecoach will turn into a pumpkin. In *The Wizard of Oz*, Glinda, the Good Witch of the North, gives Dorothy the magic formula of clicking her heels three times to get back home. "You don't need to be helped any longer," Glinda says to Dorothy. "You've always had the power to go back to Kansas." The Scarecrow, Tin Man, and Lion are amazed by the simplicity of the solution and feel as if they should have known it. "She had to find it out for herself," Glinda says. "Now those magic slippers will take you home in two seconds!"

In *Erin Brockovich*, Ed Masry advises Erin that they need additional mentors and counsel who have the expertise he lacks to win the PG&E case. In *The Bourne Identity*, Jason doesn't have a clear mentor, although one could argue that Marie, the professor, and Pamela Landy advised him what to do. In *Akeelah and the Bee*, as a coach and mentor, Dr. Larabee teaches Akeelah to be a formidable competitor so that she can not only win the Scripps National Spelling Bee, but also learn life skills that will transfer to other things.

In real life, a mentor's role is less precise yet equally pivotal and important. Mentors and models reflect the reality that we all have to learn life's lessons from someone or something. Leveraging Hollywood characters you find meaningful can be powerful. They become moving, active, living, breathing, three-dimensional mentors or models who provide more than an action plan. They evoke a tone, cadence, joie de vivre, and desirable situations and outcomes. They provide an attitude and a mindset to emulate—a character, if you will, that you can step into when your own mojo is not at 110 percent. In short, you can mirror them. You can imitate a character or actions to make your path immensely faster and simpler, your wins quicker, choices better, and progress more efficient.

Mindset mentors can be particularly potent. Frontier Business reports that 96 percent of executives consider mentorship to be a critical talent development tool. As the CEO and screenwriter of your life, you can develop your story faster and more effectively by choosing on-screen mentors. "I'm going to get my groove back like Stella; Elle Woods my way past the ex who dumped me; Erin Brockovich the shit out of that job; and finally, Joy Mangano the crap out of my new company," said one of my students. That about sums it up.

When you connect to the emotion or mindset required to achieve your goal, you call forth an untapped power. Adopting a living, breathing model for your actions and words is immensely more dynamic than starting with a blank canvas, screen, or image in your mind. Vision boards are great, but a two-dimensional picture from a magazine usually doesn't cut it. You need to see, understand, and model the full range of action, words, mindset, and emotion, adjust to your situation, and dial the level of emotion up or down depending on the circumstances.

LJ and Rocky Balboa

At eighty-five years old, while fighting cancer for more than a decade, Louis Johnson (LJ), an avid fisherman and my grandfather, modeled Rocky Balboa. In *Rocky*, the iconic scene of Sylvester Stallone running through Philadelphia in his gray sweatpants punching the air to the famous movie theme music resonated with LJ.

Rocky's on his path. He's doing the work. He's in his zone, paying his dues, and doing all he can do to reach his goal of being eyeball to eyeball with Apollo Creed and going the distance. LJ decided he was going to do that, too. He put on his gray sweatpants and regularly ran through Luxemburg, Wisconsin, punching the air, from the time he was seventy-five until he was eighty-nine, all fourteen years he battled cancer. He ran proudly, and in the spirit of a fighter. A champion. And when he told us about his runs, "punching in the air like Rocky," we knew that meant he was giving his all to stay with us just a little longer. When doctors told him what day to come in for chemo, LJ would go through his schedule and decline most of the next chemo appointments. He had to go fishing, play cards, whatever. He was busy. A hard worker. A believer. A lover of life.

Going the Distance

Mentors and role models help you make your best decisions for your greatest victories. They can swoop in like the wise elder with that one piece of critical information that puts you on an entirely different trajectory faster than you'd ever arrive at that point alone. A hero can be anyone who goes the distance. But the number one person who will go the distance for you—is you. You can have the satisfaction of grounding yourself to what's really important in your life—if you choose to. Start by figuring out what you're willing to go the distance for. And how will you go for it?

For my grandfather, Louis Johnson, his life and his family were his business. LJ was victorious over cancer for fourteen years. He probably could've inspired Rocky just as much as Rocky inspired him. No one's perfect, mostly because there's no such thing as perfection. But if you can call on the clarity and consciousness of your choices, and leverage a mentor—real or fictional—when the going gets tough, you'll end up ahead.

The Hero's Journey, a story structure created by Joseph Campbell, includes a stage called Meeting the Mentor: "At this crucial turning point where the Hero desperately needs guidance, he meets a mentor figure who gives him something he needs. He could be given an object of great importance, insight into the dilemma he faces, wise advice, practical training or even self-confidence. Whatever the mentor provides the Hero with, it serves to dispel his doubts and fears and give him the strength and courage to begin his quest."

For Tom, his mentors going up Everest were Pemba, his number one Sherpa; his coaches; brother; late friend; and an icefall doctor. My grandfather's mentor was Rocky Balboa; Maria's was the Reverend Mother. Dorothy's mentor was Glinda, the Good Witch of the North.

Mentors and models come in all shapes, sizes, and ways to help. Consider this as you plan the path to your goal, so you can get you and your loved ones up and down your version of Everest safely.

EXERCISES

1 Analyze your three past success stories from your story forensics and identify where the "ice crevasses" were. Who served in the role of your mentors, coaches, or guides, whether intentionally or unintentionally, and how, specifically, was this helpful in reaching your goal?

2 In what situations did you seek out mentors or models? In what situations were you matched with them by someone else?

3 Identify three people who could be your mentors or models for your current goal.

4 Identify three times in the past that you have given advice, served as a role model, or acted as a mentor. How did it feel to offer someone validation, resources, self-assurance?

5 Record three insights and observations from these exercises. What did you learn, remember, or realize?

At its most organized, artistic, and collaborative finest, Hollywood has formidable lessons to offer in story—to entertain, inform, and inspire the very best in each of us. Allow yourself to be informed and inspired by the very best, and treat your life and next goal as a masterful collaboration.

ANNNNND... ACTION

• • • • •

"Be brave and fearless to know that even if you do make a wrong decision, you're making it for a good reason."

ADELE

A**NNE WAS A** basket case. She hadn't slept in days. Her mom came to meet her in Chicago so they could drive together to her hometown near Dallas and spend some time in familiar surroundings. Anne grew up in Texas and was conditioned to be a Southern wife, 1950s *Good Housekeeping* style: you look nice when your husband comes home; dinner is on the table; and the children are clean and quiet.

Ovarian cancer changed some of that. Then, her husband changed the rest, in excruciating fashion. Out of the blue, he told her he had fallen in love with someone else and was leaving her. But he didn't leave, exactly. He kind of left, came back, kind of left again, came back again, sort of exited one more time, and then finally came back. The couple planned to move to California for a fresh start. So Anne quit her job in Chicago, found a new one in California, and was ready for the next chapter. But while on a boys' trip, her husband called and announced he was leaving. *Again*. That's when Anne's sleeping stopped and her mom came for support.

So the road trip began. And somewhere on the I-55 in Memphis, it became as obvious as a highway exit ramp. The years of back and forth that had weighed Anne down came into focus. She turned to her mother and said, "I can't do this."

"What are you talking about?" her mom asked.

"I'm going to drop you off at the airport in Memphis and get you a flight to Texas. But I'm going back to Chicago. And I'm going to figure this out. I'm going to stand on my own two feet, and I'm going to do it," said Anne.

Her mother looked at her as if to say, *Aw shit, she's gone crazy.*

But Anne had reached a key turning point. Her decision became clear, and she sprang into action. "I'm not going to be a miserable human being. I am going to pick myself up and do what I need to. And I'm going to live."

She dropped off her mother, drove back to Chicago, went to the bank, and withdrew half of the money in the joint account. She canceled her husband's cell phone, which she had been paying for. She had divorce papers drawn up and insisted that the divorce decree cited adultery.

Her husband was angry when he received the divorce papers. She told him, "A court date has already been set."

He was amazed. "What do you mean?"

And she said, "Dude, we're getting a divorce. You were served with the papers. So there you go. I'm not messing around anymore. You don't want to be with me. So go do your thing. Make yourself happy. I'm not gonna allow you to jerk me around anymore."

He was floored by that. And by how nice she was being. She said, "Well, it's not really about nice. I'm just letting go. I deserve more than what you can offer. So go do your thing and live with your choices. I hope that you find happiness. I hope that you find peace. I hope that you find a situation where you are fulfilled—you clearly weren't with us. And you know what? That's OK. I need somebody who loves me."

Anne marched on like the heat-packing debutante she is, and kissed the 1950s *Good Housekeeping* persona goodbye. Next up, she got a temporary apartment and sorted things out to keep her job in Chicago. A couple of months later, she signed a new lease, bought a big red couch, organized the craziest group of women friends she could find—six of them—and started hosting *Sex and the City* wine nights on Sundays. She signed up on top dating sites and created a spreadsheet for her dates. She gave them scores, ranked them, charted the position on the football team that they'd play. She said, "I came into my power. I was free to be myself."

Her weekends became "me" time and playtime with her friends, nicknamed "the gypsies." They'd usually start with brunch and then be off on any number of adventures: martini sampling, shopping at Marshall Field's, going to outdoor markets and football games... whatever crazy escapade was proposed.

Anne was on her way up and out of limbo with her husband. The catalyst was one moment of clarity, followed by a key decision, then a solid series of actions, and a fierce army of allies as reinforcements.

The Critical Juncture

Action is the intersection of your goal, desire, decisions, and movement. This is where you take the leap—just like the butterfly, which takes flight only moments after its wings form and dry. This is where all of the components of a character and her goal come together and she starts executing her plan. Likely, these components have been percolating as you've been linking things together through the exercises in the previous chapters. I see it with my coaching clients regularly. One key moment of clarity ("I can't do this") and a vision of how things could be are sometimes all it takes to set a plan in motion.

However, a vision and goal are not enough. Consider an ultramarathoner who faces one hundred miles at the start of a race. How the hell does a person approach running a hundred miles with their own feet? As someone for whom running is the equivalent of the average white guy dancing, the idea that a person would voluntarily do this absolutely blows my mind. But that's just me. Good thing you did not pick up this book for fitness counsel.

Megan Gilbert, the producer of the *Extra Ordinary* podcast, recently interviewed a series of ultramarathoners. Gilbert's conversations revealed that these athletes don't stand around before a race thinking about all one hundred miles. If they did, they'd never start. Instead, they focus solely on the mile ahead of them. And sometimes not even that far. They are sometimes thinking, "Get to that tree. Then the next tree, then the next one, and the one after that." Before they know it, they've done ten miles—literally by focusing on the trees and not the forest.

At forty-four years old, Betsy Nye ran her tenth Wasatch Front 100 Mile Endurance Run with the goal of achieving a faster race time than ever before. Using this kind of thinking, she achieved just that, finishing in less than twenty-four hours—23:15:18, to be exact—the fastest of the 2009 race and the second fastest recorded by a woman, according to the *Sierra Sun*. Extreme sports enthusiasts aren't the only ones cultivating the practice of keeping their eye on the next thing right in front of them. Gilbert says she thinks about a hundred-mile race like she does a lifetime. "You're gonna have these ups and these downs, and you have these strategies to get to the end. And you do it."

There will be points when you'll wonder what you're doing and why. "But when you keep focusing on the mini-goals," says Gilbert, "you get to what the ultrarunners call 'the high.' And after the high, they know the low will come, and [they] adjust for it."

Gilbert used this concept to get through the launch of the *Extra Ordinary* podcast in August 2018. Her personal challenges were around putting herself and her work out there. She said that like an ultramarathoner, she asked herself, "What's the next thing I need to do, and the next thing, and the next thing? Every little teeny step." Gilbert's giant leap didn't come in the form of a giant leap—it came in an accumulation of the small steps. Then, when she published *Extra Ordinary*, she didn't tell anyone for a month. She dealt with her apprehension by first allowing herself to metabolize the process and then marketing her work.

The same concepts that apply to managing an extremely difficult environment or achieving an extreme sport challenge or launching a creative endeavor also apply to your everyday goals.

Point A to Point B

In a film, scene by scene, the protagonist moves her story forward one decision and action at a time. So when you look at your goals, zero in on the same thing: a series of decisions and actions that move you from point A to point B. One at a time. Even big things happen in small steps, one by one. Some people take slow and steady decisions and actions to move forward at a consistent pace. Others do sprints and recoveries. Others let the level of discontent or discomfort rise to an unbearable tipping point, where it overflows and demands immediate action. Others fall in between, depending on the nature and circumstances of the goal.

You may feel the timing deep in your bones. You may experience a dramatic realization or a calm knowing. You might be

> **"The game is rigged, and it does not reward people who play by the rules."**
>
> RAMONA VEGA
>
> ---
>
> In a story about human nature, greed, desperation, friendship, and sisterhood, Ramona Vega is the ringleader of a squad of savvy ex-strip club employees who band together to turn the tables on their Wall Street clients. Based on actual events, the 2019 film *Hustlers* stars Jennifer Lopez as Ramona, plus Constance Wu, Keke Palmer, and Julia Stiles.
>
> Ramona's bold confidence, style, and charisma made her a successful club employee and entrepreneur. She had no patience and little regard for the Wall Street execs whom she saw as people who stole from everybody and didn't go to jail. Whatever else can be said about Ramona and her associates, one thing is clear—they were women who took action. Having a vision or goal is never enough; it's the action that generates momentum, change, and transformation in a person's story.

scared but you know it's "go" time and you must do it anyway. You've done your homework, you've prepared, and it's time to march down your path.

Ideas and goals are wonderful. Knowing your strengths and weaknesses is key. But nothing transforms a vision into reality without action. Your life is a masterpiece. Treat it like one. Give your story the thought, planning, and attention it deserves. This affects not only you but also everyone you touch.

In January 2010, humanitarian Christal Earle's plan was to finalize the adoption of her daughter in Haiti and the Dominican Republic, and return to work in Canada—a pretty straightforward point B. However, her plans became irreversibly changed when the 7.0-magnitude earthquake rocked Haiti. Everything she had prepared for with the adoption changed on a dime. The adoption agency and eventually the laws around international adoption were wiped off the map, and so was Christal's career plan.

Her point B ricocheted from international adoption to her marriage to redefining her work to not knowing where or how to start. Christal told me, "I had reached the point where I was listening to everyone else repeating to me how bad everything was, how difficult and impossible it must be, and I was choosing to believe it." Until she decided to stop believing it.

She made a conscious, actionable choice to create her future. Having worked with and learned from a local community of garbage dump workers on the North Coast of the Dominican Republic, she had shared in laughter, connection, and the hard truths about our shared humanity. The garbage dump housed a massive number of tires, which were taking up an increasing amount of space and negatively impacting the environment. Christal founded Brave Soles, a Dominican Republic–based company that upcycles these tires into the soles of shoes in an ethically produced, globally inspired line of footwear and handbags. "I have come to realize that nothing in life is certain," she said. "It's so empowering to know that I get to control the most powerful force of everything that is happening in my life: my thoughts and actions."

In the face of a constantly changing point B, Christal rises to the challenge with consistent action. Since its inception, Brave Soles has been recognized with numerous sustainable fashion awards and is growing and becoming a better business every day.

Christal commuted between Toronto and the Dominican Republic for ten years, continuing on numerous paths to complete a legal adoption and create a permanent home for her daughter.

Simplified Structure for Real Life

The way actions unfold in business and in real life are usually slower and much more organic than the way action progresses in a Hollywood film. Only the broad strokes of real life overlie screen life, so for the purposes of this book, I vastly simplified the discussion of structure.

In screenplays, key milestones happen at the following points:

- **Inciting incident:** The event/decision that sets the story in motion
- **Act 1 break:** The first major milestone the character reaches toward her goal
- **Midpoint:** Next major change that gives the character a new choice
- **Act 2 break:** Often a false victory, defeat, or requisite for the heroine to double down
- **Lost point or dark night of the soul:** When it feels that all is lost
- **Resolution:** The ultimate new world

In feature films, these points represent the major shifts in action and decisions. They also represent key victories and setbacks, which is what makes it interesting for us as the audience to follow the journey.

"There is a vitality, a life force, an energy, a quickening, that is translated through you into action, and because there is only one of you in all time, this expression is unique. And if you block it, it will never exist through any other medium and will be lost."

MARTHA GRAHAM

If your goal is to go get a hamburger at McDonald's, and you get in your car, drive two miles, cruise through the drive-through, and get your hamburger, that is not an interesting story. Now, if it's the last place on Earth to eat, and to get there you have to puddle jump on top of alligators or hotwire a helicopter for the first time, or you have to walk on one leg and put a roller-skate on the other because of an injury—*that's* a story. Otherwise, it's the "village of the happy people," as former UCLA screenwriting co-chair Lew Hunter would say, "and nobody wants to see the village of the happy people." In crafting our wildest dream, we must also keep in mind our obstacles. And as we plot action, we want to keep our eye on the prize—our key milestones: the victories that will shape our story and propel us forward.

So let's take the cue from Hollywood and use creative license to walk through your milestones, knowing they don't have to be perfect, but that they should give you a clearer picture of where you're at, where you're going, and how you're going to get there.

Remember that in Hollywood, there is no story without a goal. You too must be crystal clear on your goal. Nothing else happens without it, especially your most important action sequence. To move into choices and action, you will gather all of your exercises and place them front and center. You will review your strengths, allies, superpowers, antagonists, and weaknesses and flaws (embrace your flawesomeness), and have these things at your fingertips. You will march into action with all of it.

Your Most Important Action Sequence

Your most important action sequence is always your next one. You must stay in motion to achieve your goal. To plot your most important action sequence and beyond, you must forecast the five key milestones on your journey. Let's let the inspiration flow from our film icons.

Erin Brockovich's Key Milestones

Erin goes from broke and jobless (point A) to multimillion-dollar-earning legal advocate (point B). Her trajectory of key milestones is:

- Secures job with Masry and associates
- Goes all in and follows instinct that something's fishy in Hinkley
- Finds key evidence to prove it
- Proves she's essential to the case
- Not enough evidence to win the case, gets sick
- Resolution: Tries and wins case, earns seven-figure financial payout

Jason Bourne's Key Milestones

Jason is an amnesic assassin (point A) who becomes a crusader against the government that trained him (point B). His key milestones are:

- Gets cashed up and secures IDs
- Realizes he killed someone
- Learns he's a target for assassination
- Accesses phones and information to track Treadstone
- Puts Marie in danger
- Resolution: Reunites with Marie in Goa

Akeelah Anderson's Key Milestones

Akeelah is bullied for her school smarts (point A) and wants to win the Scripps National Spelling Bee (point B). Her key milestones along the journey are:

- Wins school spelling bee and gets Principal Welch's attention
- Agrees to coaching with Dr. Larabee on his terms
- Aligns with Javier
- Practices five thousand new words
- Is pulled out of the national spelling bee by her mom
- Resolution: Ties Devon at the Scripps National Spelling Bee—a victory for them both

It's Your Turn

As you review your goal, along with your strengths, allies, weaknesses, and so on, what appears as the most logical milestone on the path to achieving it? What can you do to move your story forward and yourself closer to your goal? If you are truly stuck, which ally can you call on to talk it through? What support—allies, resources, tools, outfit, snacks—do you need to take that one next action?

If you are pursuing a fitness goal, do you need to remove all sugar and carbs from your house? Set out your workout clothes and shoes for tomorrow? Declutter a space to do some weight training? Entirely reconceive exercise so that it's actually fun and not a chore? Figure out the most delicious things you can possibly eat and where you will source the ingredients or ready-to-eat versions on your budget?

If you are setting out to improve a relationship, do you need to ask your significant other, mother, sibling, or child out on a date or play date? Do you need to reprioritize your calendar to make time for that person? Do you need to have a difficult or vulnerable conversation? Do you have to make a first step at amends or an investment of time?

If your burning desire is to step into the fray of politics but you don't know how, do you need to do some research? Talk to some people? Go to a local meeting? Join some Facebook groups and actively ask questions? Find a mentor?

Recall my master class student Francesca, whose goal it was to write a book that would help people free themselves from their self-imposed limitations. Her action steps toward that goal were as specific as they were universal:

- Hire a writing coach
- Make writing a habit, not a choice
- Enlist an ally to read the work
- Let go of expectations
- Submit a manuscript

After rigorously completing the exercises in this chapter, Francesca concluded that, for her, failing meant "just not doing it." She needs to take credit if she succeeds at her goal, so that she can have allies without feeling that her goal is somehow lessened because of relying on them. The perspective she gained made her tire of her own excuses, of using "I'm lost" or "I'm new" or "I don't know what I'm doing" as a stalling tactic. Outlining her key steps and getting a coach neutralized her procrastination.

Gunnel, a Swedish behavioral specialist and author, identified her master class goal as finishing her next manuscript within six months of our class. Her action steps were very similar to Francesca's. Gunnel's action plan was based on her own timeline, opportunities, and obstacles, such as her heavy workload and the purchase and repair of a new house to move into during the time frame of her goal. Gunnel set herself up for success, as did Francesca, by keeping in mind other responsibilities and commitments that demanded her time. Both women's steps are concrete, actionable, and realistic for them.

You may already have ideas about your key milestones. Excellent. For inspiration, consider what has to happen before you get from your point A to your point B. If you feel unsure, list as many things as you can think of, and then you can whittle it down to the five most important items—that's what we do when writing a film!

One Frame at a Time

Your goal will be realized one action at a time—like a movie: one frame at a time, or a book: one page at a time, or a life: one moment at a time. Once you leverage your positive forces to get yourself in motion, momentum will kick in and support your action. Your next action could be:

- Making a key decision that narrows your path in some way
- Joining forces with an ally, friend, helper, coach, or mentor
- Eliminating something that's dragging you down
- Renegotiating the rules of an existing relationship at home or work
- Adjusting your environment. This could be decluttering, putting things you need in a more prominent place, or posting motivational statements where you can see them often
- Getting a badass outfit together because you know that when you look good, you feel good
- Nourishing your mindset
- Supporting your body with hydration, nutrition, exercise
- Committing to rituals that support you crossing the finish line of your goal with ease and grace

Action begets action. So you need to figure out what spurs you into action. Is it certainty, your commitment to your goal, the willingness to take a risk? Is it inspiration or motivation? Creating a support system of friends and allies? Identifying a deadline? When you are fully tuned in, clarify your next action.

EXERCISES

1 Review your three past success stories. List the five key milestones you reached for each. Don't worry if your real-life examples are things like getting off the couch or going to a certain place one day. Showing up is key.

2 Now consider your current goal. Forecast your five key milestones for it—meaning, before you reach your jackpot, anticipate what five "in-between" steps will be. This will help you break down your big journey into smaller, less intimidating steps.

3 Identify the very first thing you must do to move toward your goal.

4 Record three insights from this chapter. What lessons or observations stand out to you that could make a difference in the pursuit of your goal?

PLOT TWISTS AND THE DARK NIGHT OF THE SOUL

• • • • •

"I didn't know I had it in me. There's more to all of us than we realize. Life is so much bigger, grander, higher, and wider than we allow ourselves to think. We're capable of so much more than we allow ourselves to believe."

QUEEN LATIFAH

I STARED AT THE thirty-foot jump—the big kahuna—the seventh waterfall, peering at Mother Nature's sparkling turquoise pool below. There was just one problem: I was now terrified. The reality that I could be inducing cardiac arrest with my shenanigans felt more like a certainty than ever before.

I had finally made it to 27 Waterfalls, on my terms. Total anonymity. No cameras. All by myself. Well, all by myself in a group of three guides and seven then strangers: my own form of witness protection, perhaps. I thought I'd just go and... you know... see what happened. I thought maybe no one would really be paying attention to me, and if—um, when—I had attacks, I could maybe keep it on the down-low. No one had to be bothered. *Great plan, KP. Nice work.*

I had a panic attack at each of the first six jumps. And now, my sheer will, mental game, and internal organs were wearing down a little. I felt exhausted, but I pressed on. *The only way out is through.* As we got up to the big jump, a kind woman in the group asked if I'd be more comfortable going first. *I'll try anything*, I thought. *Obviously.*

I got up to the ledge. I must have stood there for, I don't know, ten minutes, possibly fifteen. I couldn't do it. I couldn't jump. I retreated and let the others go.

"This one's hard for everybody," a guide kindly said.

Fuck, I thought. Each new panic episode at each waterfall felt as much like an actual heart attack as the one before. *What if this doesn't work?*

The others made the big kahuna jump. Then, it was my turn to try again. Bless them: they chanted my name, clapped, shouted, cheered, and did a number of creative things to encourage and support me. I just looked down thinking, *Which one will pull me out and start CPR if this goes bad?*

I couldn't get out of my own head. I couldn't jump, but I couldn't leave this spot. *Shit. Shit. Shit. Shit.*

I thought, OK. *Change your energy.* So I turned to the guide and said, "I'm just going to look away from this for a moment and have a chat with you. At some point, then, I'll just turn and jump. OK?"

He nodded. I pivoted my body slightly to look away from the turquoise water below. I took a breath and shifted my mindset and tone.

"What's your name?" I asked.

His response: the last name on Earth I ever wanted to hear. Ever. His name represented the most traumatic experience of my life. It felt like a cosmic kick in the face. It felt like a message to run like hell. To get out of there immediately and at all costs. Any concentration and certainty I had dissipated into thin air. *This isn't right*, something inside me screamed. *I can't do this. I CAN'T do this.*

It was over.

I surrendered.

It was not going to happen that day. Weeks of work, three changed flights, extra lodging costs, time away from work; trying every imaginable sport, sequence, and contortion in the water;

panic, recovery, emotional energy: it all felt like a waste. I was devastated. The weight of disappointment nearly brought me to my knees.

The Dark Night of the Soul

The ultimate plot twist in film is the dark night of the soul, and I had arrived at mine. All was now lost. The worst thing that could possibly happen, happens: the major setback occurs, the bad guys close in, and the supreme ordeal presents itself. Whether by choice or chance, this is a time that requires courage, fortitude, and perhaps faith, as the process can lead the heroine to loneliness and despair until she finds her way out.

Shamans, medicine people, and storytellers from ancient and modern cultures around the world view the dark night of the soul as the necessity of heroines and warriors to seek a symbolic death in order to be reborn into their full potential. They see the soul's journey as never-ending, and lessons repeat in the same life as well as in multiple lifetimes.

Or, as I would say it, the dark night of the soul is the moment when after all the heroine has done to kick holy ass toward her most daring dream, everything turns into a complete shit show and she has to figure a way up, out, and through—despite every single odd, obstacle, and antagonist against her.

In my opinion, that's part of how and why we connect with Hollywood characters. We see our potential through them and in them. We feel their pain in this precious on-screen moment. We rally and we cheer her on as if our own life and future happiness depend on it.

> "Losses happen for all of us, but what matters is when you reset the pieces and play again."
> COACH KATENDE
>
> ---
>
> Phiona Mutesi has a life of constant struggle as a ten-year-old girl in Katwe, a slum in Kampala, Uganda. She becomes enchanted with the game of chess when she meets coach Robert Katende, and quickly becomes a top player in his chess group.
>
> *Queen of Katwe* is a 2016 feature film starting Madina Nalwanga as Phiona, who teaches us how chess helps us solve problems. After losing the Chess Olympiad in Russia, returning home doubtful and dejected, Phiona is about to quit chess. Ultimately, she returns to the game, wins the Chess Olympiad, becomes a Woman Candidate Master, and buys her family a home.
>
> As it does for Phiona, preparation can help you rise from the dark night of the soul and be triumphant over the obstacles that life presents, including your own lack of skill or your self-doubt.

Changing Course

The dark night of the soul may be the most formidable of obstacles, but a plot twist is not always that extreme. It can simply be the moment when the information or action changes and you are forced to make a new decision. In film, a plot twist often pushes the protagonist into a period of contemplation to figure out what to do next. New information is revealed, a new path is carved, and the heroine has a change of heart and makes an unexpected choice—she takes a risk, charts a course, says a yes or no that changes the direction of the story.

When setting out to write a 110-page screenplay, you usually have a general sense of where the story starts and ends before you begin. While writing a script, my job is to conceive what could possibly go wrong. I choose the most fitting plot twists and then write the characters into and out of them. Of course, in real life, we don't want to write ourselves into trouble... but we do want to anticipate the trouble and mitigate any discomfort and shitstorms as early as possible.

The Way Out Is Through

Let's look at some plot twists in our three movies and leverage the wisdom they have to teach us to make our own life easier. Structurally speaking, Erin Brockovich plows through more obstacles than plot twists that reverse the course of her story. Early on, she realizes that she will not have a windfall from a victorious lawsuit against the doctor that hit her car. Later, in pursuit of the PG&E case, Ed Masry partners with another, "more experienced" firm, and it seems as if Erin will have to take a back seat. But that soon comes around, as Erin is the one with the strongest relationships to the six-hundred-plus defendants. And finally, it seems she has a Category 5 stalker, who turns out to have a critical piece of evidence that can seal their case.

In his goal to recover his memory, Jason Bourne discovers he's a government assassin assigned to kill people in the name of national security. Suddenly, he doesn't want to know who he is anymore and seems fine with this decision. But his flashbacks, nightmares, and fragments of memories prod him on. Later in the story, he proceeds with the aim to disempower black op

Treadstone, the project that trained him and others and ordered the hits.

In *Akeelah and the Bee*, Akeelah lies to her mother to pursue her goal of winning the Scripps National Spelling Bee. She forges a permission slip allowing her to compete in a regional competition. But her mother finds out and pulls her out of the bee at a critical moment. Luckily, her friend and fellow competitor Javier uses every trick in the book to stall and buy Akeelah time so that she can rejoin the group and finish the competition—and she does.

So what do these films tell us about how to prepare for the crazy shit that can possibly happen? Although some could argue that it's a personal decision, my approach when taking on the biggest and most important of life goals is to overprepare. That's what makes me feel most ready to go into battle, as if I've done my homework and thought of all the possibilities. Of course, sometimes that's just not possible, but doing this work—the exercises in this book—prepares you with at least a starting point of resources to tap into if or when something hits the fan.

Find the Gold

Also, not all plot twists are bad. They can lead us to the next thing if we stay on our path.

Mike, a master class student, is a business owner in his mid-thirties, a husband and father of two, and a blue belt in jiu-jitsu. He got a wild hair to compete in the International Brazilian Jiu-Jitsu Federation World Championship. He was very clear that he wanted to compete in the open division, not the senior division. Getting to the competition was his goal. "I didn't expect to get really far," Mike said. "I just wanted to compete in the

"You aren't what you accomplish, you are what you overcome."

JULIA ALVAREZ

tournaments to say I did it. To lose weight, to train, to not be injured, to make it out of training at the right weight." His "going the distance" was being able to get in the ring with any fighter of any age. He did not want to cop out.

To do so, he had to overcome his lack of experience and conflicting priorities to train and compete in front of thousands of spectators. After substantial training, conditioning, and preparation to meet all of the requirements of his weight class and the competition, he registered. But then, to his astonishment, he learned that competitors had to weigh in immediately before competing wearing their *gi* (uniform). In regional competitions, you can weigh in naked and hours before the fight.

Mike was already two pounds over for his weight class; the official scale is usually one to two pounds off, balancing out his overage, but the *gi* weighs five pounds. No way could he risk being off by seven pounds, and reducing calories would hurt his strength and recovery. He had to increase both his calories and cardio to make the weight. At the last minute, he also found a four-pound *gi*.

"I was super-paranoid that I'd miss weight," Mike said. He wanted to be two pounds lighter to make absolutely sure he could fight. When the time came, he stepped onto the scale and had another huge surprise—he was six pounds underweight. Wishing he'd had a few more cheeseburgers, he stepped up to face a full-time fighter from Las Vegas, and thought, *I'm an old married dude with a full-time job and two kids.*

This was a one-time all-or-nothing fight. Six minutes. One match. Two minutes in, he was holding his own. Three minutes in, an even score. Four minutes in, it was still 0–0. Finally, Mike was caught in a choke hold that cut off the blood flow in his carotid artery. None of his countermoves were working. He was about to pass out, but before he did, he tapped out.

At first, he was sad and disappointed; he felt bad that he lost his very first match. He felt like he'd let down his coach and friend who flew in to the event to see him. But then, nobody cared that he lost—not even his kids. Later, it sunk in that he had achieved his goal.

"I reached a goal of being on that stage and in that place, and *that* was a success." Mike was fifteen pounds lighter and in great shape, and he had learned a great deal in his training—"a lot of intangible things that I didn't really realize till afterward," he said. "I lost the fight, but I came out so much further ahead than if I had not done the tournament. It was so cool to prove to myself that I could do it."

Specifically, Mike learned the move that lost him the tournament: the bow and arrow choke hold. He went on to use it relentlessly in future competitions. Ultimately, Mike said that the experience was a win, because it pushed him further than he thought he could go. He mined the gold from the situation.

Anticipate Risks and Barriers

"The notion of anticipating barriers and risks is a great way to make any plan more comprehensive and increase the probability of success," Mike told me. "It also reveals weaknesses that you can address before they turn into major issues."

Anticipating potential obstacles and risks in advance helps you have a better plan and more certainty. When you think through what can possibly go wrong, you can take steps to neutralize those things. In everyday life, it's the packing of extra gluten-free granola bars, water, and cell phone batteries for the car, train, plane, or trail. When we attempt bigger or new things, thinking through potential obstacles enables us to head them off at the pass and take different or more savvy steps sooner to be more comfortable, feel more confident, and, ultimately, create a more successful outcome.

Another of my master class students, Jeanette, wanted to be a visionary thought-leader and sought-after wellness advocate. She had survived much loss because of health challenges and was committed to making a difference in other people's lives. In considering the path to her goal, she identified some formidable potential plot twists:

- Getting rejected from conferences
- Being unable to secure clients
- Receiving a job offer that she could not refuse

The weakest link in her story at this point was her need for money. Recently divorced and having lost both parents, she had a valid and universal fear for her survival. But the mere exercise of identifying potential plot twists led Jeanette to envision some possible outcomes should the worst of her plot twists happen:

- She throws all caution to the wind and starts being more of her badass self, and people love it. She has the idea to pivot to the subject matter of self-relationship instead of health.
- She finds an investor for her health and wellness company who helps her grow it into one of the largest wellness-training and employee-health-benefit companies/programs.

Jeanette said that her fear made her alert but also irrational. "I make choices out of trying to find something that works instead of sticking to what I believe in until it works," she said. Can you relate?

For a film to be dynamic and successful, the heroine is written into a hopeless, impossible corner, where she is furthest from reaching her goal and it appears that all hope is lost. But we don't have to be so serious or melodramatic here. At least, I seriously hope not, friends. What is important is that we think through and calculate what the obstacles might be and what could possibly go wrong, including our own beliefs and mindset. We don't want to dwell on it. At the same time, we do want to be prepared and have an idea of what extra allies and resources might be needed to overcome these potential plot twists in our game plan. This is about being prepared, not paranoid. It's about being confident in your plan and anything that you may encounter on your way.

EXERCISES

1 Revisit your past success stories. Write down the plot twists for each. How did you navigate them? What new information was revealed and what new choices did you make as a result?

2 Review your current goal and related elements. Forecast one to three plot twists. What's the weakest link in the chain? Don't worry about doing anything about that right away. For now, just consider what could go wrong, and what information or change in status could present itself.

3 List three observations about your experience with the subject of plot twists.

This is about knowing your risks and building a plan so you are armed with confidence that you can handle anything that comes up. We'll get you suited up in Kevlar, figuratively, in chapter 14.

THE SUPREME ORDEAL

• • • • •

"What you need to know is, nobody can save you or heal you. Only you can do that for you."

JENNIFER LOPEZ

IT WAS OVER. I stood at the thirty-foot waterfall, six panic attacks into the day, desperate for a breakthrough. But I could not bring myself to make this jump. I couldn't do it.

In the movie version of this moment, this is where the weight of disappointment would buckle my knees, rendering me a sobbing heap on the ground, telenovela style.

What actually happened was, I took a step away from the ledge. And in that moment, time froze and everything went into slow motion. As the front of my foot crunched the ground, I heard a voice, crystal clear.

This is not who I fucking am.

On that same single step, I pivoted back to the ledge.

Again, I stood above the big kahuna waterfall and looked down.

And then... *I jumped!!*

It happened that fast. As if I were compelled. No time to think.

I jumped for myself. I jumped for my past, for my future, and for all that I believed to be good and holy. And guess what? Underwater, I thought I might have... you know... crossed over. It was so quiet. Like, super-creepy, horror-movie quiet. But also not. It was also peaceful. Wait—was it quiet because *I wasn't panicking*? I wasn't panicking. When I came up for air, I was breathing... evenly and with tranquility. And the small crowd of my new friends cheered as if we had all won the World Cup.

Something took over. My subconscious? My higher self?

Friends, I have come to know what I will share with you now. It was my ego.

The Big Deal about the Supreme Ordeal

The Supreme Ordeal, part of Joseph Campbell's Hero's Journey, is defined as the moment the heroine faces her biggest challenge—which could be the dark night of the soul, as it was for me—and is ultimately reborn. This rebirth is what enables the heroine to complete her journey—it's what will ultimately get us (shove us, thrust us, or otherwise lead us) to our point B.

This is the moment when the heroine uses everything she's got to get herself out of that plot twist or dark night of the soul and into a new reality. The clincher: this is only possible if every single component of what we've reviewed—the SMART goal, character DNA, back story, strengths, flawesomeness, allies, antagonists, mentors, action, bulletproofing, and all of the choices, chances, changes, and actions are fully leveraged, right here and now. The Supreme Ordeal doesn't happen to you—it happens for you, when you've taken action to create it.

And guess what? This works in film, as it does in real life, when our homework is done and the boxes are ticked. Why? Because to be successful, you have to properly nourish your subconscious, so that when you are faced with that ultimate confluence, your subconscious is prepared—it's scripted, if you will, for how to deal with it.

The cosmic confluence of everything you've done up to this point is what creates the momentum that propels you forward to rebirth.

In screenwriting, we often say, "Let the characters write the story." Well. If we apply this to real life, we are the screenwriter and the character. It's a little meta, but suffice it to say, if you've laid the groundwork prescribed in these chapters, you'll be good to go. What's important to learn from this is that when you are attempting your wildest dream, all the work you have done to this point will serve in your favor. You have fed your subconscious by doing every exercise to prepare for this exact moment.

What the Ego Has to Do with It

The ego demands our attention through negative emotions. Our instinctive reactions to feelings such as fear, guilt, anger, angst, or sadness give the ego a bad rap. Of course, we think of the ego as "bad" when we see people or find ourselves upset, yelling, withdrawing, or fighting. These are our instincts, responding this way to protect us.

"The ego is not our enemy," says Fernanda Rocío González Soto, "Nascanam," Chamán de las Américas (a shaman of the Americas), a spiritual coach I've had the pleasure of working with. Instead, she says that our pain alerts us, through negative, disempowering emotions, to a deep wound that needs healing.

The ego is our spotlight. It's the filter of our conscious mind. It shows us what we have to work on in ourselves in order to evolve. It builds our personality and identity. Our purpose is to evolve through our experiences. Making changes in our life centers on the ability to harness our ego. This means tempering our reactive, instinctive nature by pausing to make conscious choices. When our ego becomes present or prominent, it is showing us a wound that needs to be healed so that we can move forward in our life. The ego illuminates the thing that needs our attention and commands our focus through negative emotions. We can push through: we want and need to heal that wound.

Remember Bill, the gent who wanted to play drums with Fleetwood Mac? He dove in after his wildest dream where others would've halted and said, "How can I possibly do that when I don't have a home—or a job?" Or, "How can I make the right decision when I don't even know if I'm going to eat tonight?" "How do I recover from this loss/trauma/heartache/health issue/financial setback and rebuild a life I'm excited about?" Maybe he was driven by his ego, and maybe I was, too. A light shined on what was truly missing for us—on the thing we needed most.

Both Fernanda and I, through our respective work, help people make more conscious decisions. To do that, we need to examine what gets in the way of conscious choices. When disempowering situations arise, our instincts kick in and our emotions revert to autopilot. Instinct leads us to fear, anger, and sadness: the "Triangle of Disempowerment."

Alligator Wrestling Negative Thoughts

Fernanda explains that the Triangle of Disempowerment is used in shamanic and ancient healing as the foundation for—well, basically everything. The triangle refers to the three most disempowering feelings: fear, anger, and sadness. These emotions stem from our past and present trauma. The primary wound of human beings can always be traced back to one thing: the lack of love. Love that was given and then taken away, love that ended suddenly, love that was never given at all, not enough love, love that was desired but not received. Love. It's all about love, all the time.

So when a lack of love triggers our ego to shine a light on a deep wound, usually subconsciously, our instinct will kick in and harness our attention, using fear, anger, or sadness. If we don't check ourselves by pausing, these negative emotions and the personas they feed into will run our show, often subconsciously. Where the ego is present, it is illuminating our wound, giving us a disempowering experience that nudges us to discomfort, then pain—and ultimately, to change.

Each of the three disempowering emotions corresponds with one of three personas, in no particular order. When we feel anger, it means we are triggered by abandonment or helplessness. To protect ourselves, we respond as an aggressor. The second persona in the triangle is ruled by sadness, feeling incapable, or as if we are not enough. In this case, we respond as the victim. The third persona is ruled by fear and guilt, often as a result of feeling invalidated. In this case, we show up as the savior. An article by Marissa Levin in *Inc.* magazine reports the aggressor, the victim, and the savior as the three most dangerous roles in leadership.

So the ego does its job by harnessing our attention with a disempowering experience. This experience drives our instinctive negative emotions from a point in the triangle. In this moment, we are wired to react, but we must learn to pause and choose a better response.

The internal voice I heard saying "This is not who I fucking am" was my ego, shining a light on my anger and frustration from my deep wound that needed healing. In the pause that was the step I took away from the ledge, I pushed past the victim and aggressor mode into positive action—because I wanted and needed to heal that wound.

This moment represents my supreme ordeal: the confluence of my goal, my soul-level desire, my character DNA, strengths, flawesomeness, allies, mentors, and antagonists, including my ego, battling it out up there on the ledge.

With emotional intelligence and the exercises throughout this book, we can re-empower ourselves. When we are able to clearly identify our negative experience, we can then pause, intercept, and make a conscious choice, instead of staying stuck in a disempowering loop. So where we want to get to when we feel sad, angry, or afraid is to a pause. A pause allows us to take a breath and consciously choose our next step, instead of reacting instinctively with anger, sadness, or fear. To get the bigger picture, when we feel regularly "alerted" by negativity, we can track our responses to everyday situations. Over time, this information enables us to see our patterns and identify our deeper wounds.

Fernanda trains youth in this foundation, the triangle, at InspireDR, an organization that teaches practical life skills and instills positive values in Dominican boys. She is having incredible outcomes as the boys learn about themselves, their reactions, and how to make conscious choices. As a result, she is seeing scholarship opportunities and less fighting where it is known to be prominent and even expected behavior. She reminds us, "The ego is not our enemy. It shows us what we have to work on about ourselves to evolve."

Remember Michelle Bourdeau's story, when her award for winning first place in a windsurfing competition was less than one-tenth of the men's first-place prize? Her instinctive reaction to the unfairness was anger—and to get revenge. Understandable. But this was also constrictive, and she felt that. She was able to let it pass, sought out a better decision, and found it. Her choice was to create an experience that focuses on women in the water. She put her project, modeled after Tatiana Howard's Butterfly Effect, into motion; 2021 will celebrate its thirteenth year of empowering some one thousand women. That is a choice made out of love. That is a choice that is expansive.

> **Attorney: "Ready to go to war?"**
> **Gretchen Carlson: "Oh yeah. I'm ready."**
>
> ---
>
> The 2019 film *Bombshell* details the true story of three intelligent, ambitious, strong women who anchored one of America's most powerful news networks and became headlines themselves when they risked everything to stand up against the man who made them famous.
>
> Starring Nicole Kidman as Gretchen Carlson, Charlize Theron as Megyn Kelly, and Margot Robbie as composite character Kayla Pospisil, the three women face career suicide by going public about the atrocious, systematized sexual harassment by Fox network head Roger Ailes. It takes a confluence of allies, circumstances, and standing together to push through an avalanche of disempowerment and take this very public and far-reaching supreme ordeal into the spotlight, which in turn sets an example for numerous others facing sexual harassment.
>
> In order for a supreme ordeal to materialize, you must be willing to leave your ordinary, often safe world, be willing to trust your strengths and superpowers, and traverse uncertain and uncharted territory to create the world you want.

The Ultimate Fuel

I hope you do not have to face a choice of surrendering to defeat or risking literal or figurative harm or death to make progress toward your goal. No matter how high your stakes are, dear reader, my sincerest wish is that you have done the work laid out in this book. Because the clarity and confidence it will evoke, whether or not you realize it, will burrow into your subconscious and serve you when you need them most.

This is important because your subconscious rules 95 percent of your brainpower. According to an article by Brenda Berg, "by taking control of your subconscious mind, by becoming aware and in sync with it, you can be sure to take back control of your life and basically achieve anything you want to. This is because when your subconscious mind and your conscious mind is [sic] working together to achieve a common goal, you can believe that it will happen." Further research, by Joydeep Bhattacharya at Goldsmiths, University of London and Bhavin Sheth at the University of Houston, looks at how our brains solve problems: "It shows that our brain solves problems many seconds before we become consciously aware of the solution!"

I was convinced that subconscious mojo was at play for me at waterfall number seven, where I stood unable to move, where I finally walked away, and where I pivoted on that one step away and took the leap that changed my life. The way Fernanda saw it, first my ego triggered my debilitating fear, and then my subconscious, or higher consciousness, quelled that fear and convinced me I would be OK. To me, it felt as though my fear and my higher consciousness had a wrestling match at the ledge, and my higher consciousness, or soul, won.

EXERCISES

1. Do a ten-day emotional triangle inventory. Track your disempowering emotions for ten days and see what patterns you notice. Track four things:

   - Date/time of day
   - Event
   - Emotion (fear, anger, sadness)
   - Role (savior, aggressor, victim)

2. Journal on these questions:

   - What patterns do you notice?
   - What instinctive reactions did you have? What did you do?
   - What conscious choices did you make?
   - If you could be more conscious of these triggers, how would you prefer to respond on a regular basis?
   - What would be the benefit to you overall? How would that change your level of empowerment?

3. Analyze your three past success stories. What was the moment of confluence—your supreme ordeal—in them? Which components were the biggest contributors to moving the needle to success in each story? Notice any patterns?

4. Review your past success stories. On a scale of 1-10, how committed to your goal were you?

5. Think about your current goal. What elements that you've outlined in this book could you double down on to increase your

chances for success? On a scale of 1-10, how committed to this goal are you?

6   Revisit your current goal. Take another pass at your timing: How realistic does it feel? If necessary, adjust it so that it's so doable, it's almost impossible not to see yourself winning.

LOVE CONQUERS ALL

· · · · ·

"If grass can grow through cement, love can find you at every time in your life."

CHER

LOVE CONQUERS ALL.

I've always loved the phrase "love conquers all." I know some people think it's cheesy. I don't care. I like the sound of it. I like the idea of it. I like the concept that love is our ultimate strength and elixir and can truly overcome everything. Also, it's proven by science.

"Love conquers all" applies when we think about going after our next wildest dream. Because—if you'll recall the work of Dr. David Hawkins that we discussed in chapter 8—the opposite of love is not hate: it's fear. Fear won't get us closer to our goal, but love will. Self-love, decisions that come from a place of love, actions that are fueled by love, and a deeper connection to our goal and mission through love will propel us forward. Fear and its cousins, anger and sadness, on the other hand, will get our attention, but they will not, on their own, propel us forward. We'll need to add some love to the mix to be the victor here. You with me?

Hawkins's work shows us, with some math, how important it is to work through disempowering emotions. Although our ego will go low with the force of an ocean undertow, when we consciously choose love and peace, these feelings displace everything else. Love and fear cannot exist in the same place.

Albert Einstein wrote a letter to his daughter, Lieserl, about the monumentally powerful, universal driving force behind any phenomenon: love. He compares love to his famous $E=mc^2$ equation, but says that because it is limitless, it is the most powerful force there is. The letter was donated to The Hebrew University of Jerusalem in the late 1980s, and includes the statement, "When we learn to give and receive this universal energy... we will have affirmed that love conquers all."

Our Heart's Desire

Fear and anxiety are emotions that cause us to contract. They make us think, decide, and act in a smaller way. They keep us stuck.

Love, on the other hand, allows us to live an expansive life. But we have to be open, even just a crack, to the possibility. That is our job, our work in a moment when fear and doubt try to steal the show. All we need is to see the possibility. Love will then conquer the doubt.

Executive leadership coach and spiritual advisor Gail Angelo told me in an interview, "Do you see that if love conquers all and if we just open the door a bit to it, that's expansive? And that expansion pushes the door a little more and a little more until we are living a full and all-embracing life, without judgment and with compassion. There is no love without compassion and there's no compassion without love." Self-compassion is a key component of love, which is why I talk about observing, not judging, in this book. We can have strengths and superpowers and flex them. We can have flaws and accept them. We can face obstacles and overcome them, but to accomplish that, to infuse that into our character DNA, we must practice self-love and self-compassion.

> "I wouldn't change what happened to me
> because then I wouldn't have this chance,
> in front of all of you, to embrace more people
> than I ever could have with two arms."
>
> BETHANY HAMILTON

The 2011 film *Soul Surfer* details the true story of thirteen-year-old competitive surfer Bethany Hamilton, who lost an arm to a 1,500-pound tiger shark and had to rediscover her balance on the board in order to surf again.

In the movie, which features AnnaSophia Robb as Bethany Hamilton; Dennis Quaid and Helen Hunt as her supportive parents, Cheri and Tom Hamilton; and Carrie Underwood as Sarah Hill, a mentor, ally, and leader of a local youth group, Bethany summons faith and courage to face what's next after her accident. Sidelined by the difficulties of surfing with one arm, Bethany travels to Thailand to volunteer after the devastating 2004 tsunami. While there, she reconnects with her love of the water and finds her bigger purpose—to make a difference in the lives of others.

Bethany surrounds herself with love—for the water, for her sport (her ultimate goal), and for her family, faith, and friends. Back home on Kauai, she is even more committed to surfing and ultimately beats a six-time world champion and wins multiple competitions.

"Showing up in
love is like dessert."

GAIL ANGELO

Love is a melting mechanism, Gail told me. Love has the power to thaw the iceberg of panic. We must look inside ourselves for what has held us too tight for so long—the internal icebergs. We must pay attention to where we feel contracted—this shows us where we could expand. "If we can open ourselves to the idea of love, and that it's possible love conquers all, then the melting begins," said Gail.

This doesn't mean that we're wearing rose-colored glasses. It means we're choosing to say, "I'm smart, I'm capable, I'm resilient." It means we ask better questions, like, "How do I want to think about this differently? What *can* I do?" These are questions derived from love.

In Gail's experience, many people don't think or practice the thought that they have choice. "We're trained to protect ourselves. But our natural way of being is just the opposite," Gail said. The constrictive approach is to say, "I can't." An expansive approach is, "So what can I do?" You need to sit down for a second and make a list of all the things you know you can do.

My personal tendency (hello again, flawesomeness!) is to try to translate this into, "What am I doing?" and put it in the context of my tasks, schedules, commitments, and plans. But Gail said that's not the question. The real question is, "How do I approach this from a place of expansion?" The clarity is in expansion. "We need to show up for our goals from the *being* place of ourselves, not the intellect or doing place," Gail told me. When we're not in the being, we're in the doing, and that is constrictive.

When you make decisions and choose actions of love, you are supporting the expansion of who you are so that you can be of greater service to your own purpose and to the world.

Let's look at the influence of love in our film icons' stories.

Erin is initially driven by her love for her children and herself. As she delves into the PG&E case, her love and care for the

Hinkley residents expands her commitment and mission. She is also influenced by her desire for justice in this story.

Jason is compelled to find his true identity, which is further influenced by his romance with Marie and also his reflection about the two children in the farmhouse where he hides out, as well as the children who appear in his flashbacks. His former life as a covert government assassin is constrictive, and he desires expansion—running away from it. He takes action, risking his life and loss, to keep Marie and the children safe.

Akeelah was self-directed by her love of words and language, which was further amplified by her love for her father and her coach's attention and commitment to helping her. Making friends at the spelling competitions added another layer of love, of a shared activity, and as she pursued this goal and felt the support of unexpected allies, she developed love for herself.

We can see how all of our characters' tangible goals are tied to a higher purpose—to their deeper "why" beyond their immediate goal. Mine was, too. Like Bethany Hamilton, I loved the water. I grew up on it. And though I'm not a professional water woman, I share this love of swimming and playing in the water with my niece and nephew. Love is expansive. Remember that our brain's reticular activating system is wired in our favor—when we focus on our goal, when we focus on love, the RAS will work to make connections for us. Saying our first yes to ourselves helps us get moving toward our goal.

Recalling that the subconscious mind works one thousand times faster than the conscious mind, I'm sure that a deeper motivation, my internal why, kicked in during my supreme ordeal on the ledge of the seventh waterfall, and that also contributed to me taking the leap. Love conquered all of my inner obstacles that day: self-love, love for the water, and love for my niece and nephew and my deep desire to swim with them any time, any place, for the rest of our lives.

In film, the writer has to be deeply in touch with the character's "hierarchy of why" in every moment of every scene. And just as with real-life characters, that information is relayed in layers. Erin Brockovich wants to follow her calling because she wants to take better care of her family. And she wants to be more in life. Jason Bourne wants to recover his memory because he's lost without it. And he wants to find his true self. Akeelah Anderson wants to win the national spelling bee because she realizes her unique ability and wants to develop and use her gift to its fullest potential.

Focus on one question and one question only. What do you want—now—and why?

OK, that's two questions. Also, where is the love in what you want? Three questions.

So, what do you want and why, and where is the love in it?

Sit with it. Be still with it. Meditate on it. Walk with it. Dance with it. Talk to it. If you're still not sure, double down. Turn on *The Notebook* and watch the scene in which Allie and Noah are reunited and Noah asks Allie four times in a row, "What do you want?" each time emphasizing a different word in the question, imploring Allie to answer for herself, and not for him, her fiancé; not for her mother. For her and her alone. You need to do the same. And I'd argue you need to do it at every crossroad of every real-life action sequence to keep yourself on track to achieving your ultimate purpose.

Remember also to identify where the love is in your want. When you are clear and connected to your why, every action is faster and more on point. It's as if you are aligning your soul's compass, so that if your mindset fails in the moment of truth, your deep connection will take over and guide you. When Dorothy landed in Munchkinland, she wanted to get back home. Her why was her family. It was everyone she loved and everything she knew. There was only one thing to do and she did it. She trotted right down that yellow brick road, belting out a tune, no qualms about it. That's the kind of certainty I want for you, too.

Uncertain, on the other hand, is a swamp town in Texas. Population ninety-four. No one really wants to live in Uncertain, and I don't suggest it for you, either.

When you are truly connected to your why in a blood-oath-pinkie-swear-in-a-treehouse kind of way, you can cut through metric tons of bullshit in one fell swoop. Guess where those metric tons of bullshit land when you are not intimately connected to your why? Bingo: on all sides of you in a toxic sheath, keeping you from your goal—like that moment when I said I couldn't do it and stepped away from the ledge.

Your why will pull you back like the force of gravity. Your why informs every step in your plan. It serves as the traffic light and gives you the clear green when it's time to go. To know why is to have clarity. To have clarity increases your decisiveness, and this makes taking action easier.

Your why must go beyond the obvious and into the heart and soul of your goal. For Bill, who wanted to play drums with Fleetwood Mac, I imagine his internal why was to really live. Having housing and a job were necessities for living, but he wanted a *life*. For me, I started to worry I would have panic attacks in the shower. But also, being in and near the ocean is where I am happiest and most at peace. I felt something was deeply missing without swimming in my life, and it's a special activity I share with my niece and nephew.

Q: Why is freedom important?
A: Because one of my soul's deepest longings is for freedom, and I always want to have a choice about how I live and what I do.

Q: Why?
A: Because choices mean freedom. I want my niece and nephew, who also love the water, to also always enjoy that same feeling of freedom, and for us to have fun in the water together.

You can see that the theme for me is freedom and living fully, never again returning to the dark night of the soul. I am often asked how in the world I could do such an outlandish thing as jump into 27 Waterfalls to overcome panic attacks in the water. I often respond, how could I not? Always, always remember that you and only you have the power to rewrite your narrative at any moment in time.

EXERCISES

1. Explore your why. Go deeper and do the Six Circles of Why as a written exercise. If it's unclear, talk through the Six Circles of Why with a partner who won't take any bullshit.

2. Take one more pass at all the reasons, both internal and external. Got 'em all? Any last additions? Give yourself the space to meditate on your why and connect to it.

3. Analyze the decisions and actions from your three past successes. Where was the love? Your self-love, your love for your goal or cause, your love for or from others? Write it down.

4. Do the same analysis on your current goal: list all the sources the love *could* come from—even the unexpected places.

5. Journal on this question from Gail: If I loved myself, what would I do? How would I care for myself? Does the idea of this choice/action/next step make me feel expansive or constricted?

Then, get ready for action.

BULLETPROOFING

"Sometimes, what you're looking for is already there."

ARETHA FRANKLIN

AT HIS ONE HUNDREDTH birthday party on April 28, 2019, Noel Zeldin, my bonus grandfather, said these words: "People have come up to me and said, 'Noel, how do you do it? How do you look so well and stand so well and talk so well? What's the secret?' And I thought very hard. And I said, 'The formula is lots of sex and lots of booze.'" The audience howled with laughter. Noel followed with his rendition of the song, "Young at Heart."

I interviewed Noel the next day: a man with such a warm heart, an easy laugh, a razor-sharp sense of humor, and resilience to be admired. Unprompted, he told me that if I gave him $100 million, he'd have to give it away. He couldn't use it. At one hundred years old, that's a sign of a life well lived. Here's his story about the decision that launched his business career, the twists and turns that followed, and his lessons in bulletproofing.

In 1945, when Noel was twenty-six years old, he decided to pass by his brother Sam's house. They were the youngest of eight kids, and Sam was Noel's hero: clever, witty, and extremely artistic.

"Geez, these are nice lamps," Noel said as he stood in the living room of his brother's Toronto apartment.

"Yeah, I just made them," Sam replied.

"You know, I could sell these things," said Noel. At the time, he was working as a bookkeeper for a clothing manufacturer. "I could sell these things to somebody. Eaton's or Simpsons." Two of the largest department stores in Canada.

"Awww, you're crazy," Sam said, brushing it off.

"Nope, I'm gonna. I'm gonna try," said Noel. He had never sold anything in his life.

So the next day, Noel walked into Eaton's. He had no idea how this was typically done. After questioning various people, he was introduced to Sadie, the buyer for the lamp department. She bought twelve lamps.

"I didn't even know how to price the damn thing," Noel said. "I had to put a price on it, and it was ten dollars or twelve dollars."

When Noel told his brother the news, Sam said they could make the lamp bases in their father's garage and buy the shades. So the brothers made the lamps part time, working at night with the help of their wives.

"Maybe I should go to Montreal," Noel thought. So he played hooky from his job one Saturday, took the train, arrived at noon, and walked into Eaton's in Montreal. This isn't how sales were done, Noel told me. "That's the beauty of ignorance."

At the end of the day, Noel sent a telegram to his brother: "We have to quit our jobs or quit this business. I have six more orders." He had sold more lamps to Eaton's and Simpsons, as well as Morgan's, Ogilvy's, and others in Montreal. The brothers quit their jobs, rented workshop space, and launched the lamp business, as well as Noel's business career—full time.

Soon, they outgrew their rented space. There was just one problem: their work with wood, papers, and lacquers made them an extreme fire hazard, and they couldn't find a new space. Nobody wanted them as a tenant. It was late 1947.

"We were as busy as sons of bitches," Noel remembered. "So we said, well, the hell with it, we'll build our own building. So we started building this building, and we forgot one thing. We didn't have enough money."

They couldn't get help from the bank. They couldn't qualify for a mortgage. They were in a real pickle. But then they realized there was one thing that would fly: they could sell the partially finished building. So they did—for a $20,000 profit. "At that time [1948], $20,000 was a huge amount of money," Noel said. In 2020, the amount is comparable to approximately Can$240,000 (or US$172,000).

Next, they built two more buildings—one for the lamps and another as a development. They made another $20,000 selling one of these buildings when just the basement was in. Then, they had an aha moment: they were in the wrong business. They couldn't sell the lamp-making outfit because it was a specialty business, but they sold the building and their equipment for $30,000. And then they went into the building business.

Noel and Sam built apartments and other buildings for several years on their own. Later, they joined forces with three other companies to form Consolidated Building Corporation, and grew it to be the largest home building company in Canada at the time. After ten years, the brothers parted ways with the other partners. Sam and Noel continued to work together until 1980 building their own stuff. Noel bought a piece of land on Yonge Street, the longest street in Canada and also in a very desirable area. He flipped it for a great profit, which allowed him to retire in the late '80s, when he was in his early sixties. "So, just going to my brother's apartment started my business career," Noel said.

Noel's story underscores two things. First, the power of having a single focal point and keeping an adventurous mindset. He

"When coming up with your happy ending, drink from the firehose of possibility."

ANONYMOUS

started with an appreciation and an entrepreneurial spirit, a "let's try and see what happens" attitude with the lamps. He couldn't have predicted on that day that he'd end up a successful real estate developer, but that's where his curiosity, nimble mindset, and enterprising qualities blazed the way. My original question to Noel was, "What was a decision that changed your life?" And his answer was going to his brother's place on a random night, for no particular reason. It's a reminder for us to do just the very next thing on our journey, not the next thousand steps. Who are you visiting tonight? Where is the love?

Noel's story also underscores the power of our character strengths, allies, and openness to having fun on the journey. His curiosity, nimbleness, and enterprising spirit made his plan bulletproof, as did his zest for life. "Let's try and see what happens": a great motto for life.

Often, when I'm deciding what to do, I hear that in my head. It's maybe less of a strategy and more of a mindset, but there you go. It's Kevlar for the mind.

In theory, that might seem like a rather flexible definition of bulletproofing, which may instead conjure up the image of a thick, rigid shield, harder than nails. However, as Noel Zeldin, Verna Johnson, and Kevlar show us, there's more than one way to be bulletproof.

Stronger Than Steel

Stronger than steel—that's how Kevlar is described. Kevlar is a lightweight fiber used to make bulletproof vests. In technical terms, it's known as poly-paraphenylene terephthalamide, and it was invented by Polish-American chemist Stephanie Kwolek, while she worked for DuPont in 1965. Kevlar's original, commercial use was as a replacement for steel in racing tires. It is also used for racing sails, marching drumheads, mooring lines and other underwater applications, and, of course, bulletproof vests.

I don't know why I have this affection for Kevlar, but I do. Perhaps it relates to when I was developing The Hollywood Approach, teaching medical professionals in Canada how to leverage characters like Jason Bourne to achieve their outcome: patient-focused medicine. At that time, I had this jacket that looked like a vest. The vest part was mango-colored—in a very interesting, almost plastic-like material—and the arms were a woven light gray. My first day on the job, the CEO asked me why I was wearing Kevlar. And it kind of stuck.

Since we're all cozy here and you're up on my mango jacket couture from 2012, allow me to geek out about the science of material strength. These nerdy tests show that Kevlar is five times stronger than steel. And this is about the same level of badassery at which I want your Hollywood Approach game plan to be.

When a material breaks sharply, it's called a brittle failure. If that term doesn't conjure up something breaking into a million pieces never to come back together again, I don't know what does. Brittle failure. *Ew*. The sound of these two words together makes me shudder. A brittle failure is what happens when we don't have a plan—or the real or virtual Kevlar to back it up. Hear me when I say, again, like the chorus of your very favorite song, I want the badass rating of your game plan to be five times stronger than steel. If one of you reading this is a composer, I welcome the creation of a jingle of that. "I want your game plan to be *five times* stronger than steel... I want it to be—bulletproof."

Let's talk about how we do that.

> **"This is just the beginning."**
>
> RUTH BADER GINSBURG
>
> ---
>
> Ruth Bader Ginsburg was the second female associate justice of the United States. In part because of her trademark outspokenness, she became a feminist folk hero, and was given the nickname "Notorious RBG." The 2018 biographical drama *On the Basis of Sex*, starring Felicity Jones, follows RBG through her first groundbreaking case in which the outcome overturns a century of gender discrimination.
>
> This story illustrates how Ruth made consistently savvy, conscious choices to put herself in the path of opportunities to fight for the causes she believes in. She takes special care to curate the best allies and advice, and by knowing and leveraging her strengths, she becomes a leading figure and advocate for women's rights and gender equality. You, too, can bulletproof your game plan with preparation, amping up your allies and doubling down on your strengths and superpowers. You've got this.

Figurative Kevlar

First, a moment of truth: there's no official concept or practice of "bulletproofing" in screenwriting. I totally made this up for my own vices and devices. To me, bulletproofing is the practice of wrapping a figurative layer of Kevlar around your most vital ideas, plans, resources, timing, allies, and so on. Bulletproofing is about going the extra five miles on the risks and investments you've already made to give yourself the best shot at the best outcome. It's doubling down, tripling down, and going all in. Bulletproofing comes into play when you've used up 100 percent of your courage and then you have to reach for 20 percent more. When you have prepared 100 percent and then do 25 percent more. It's that extra boost that will differentiate you, protect you from random plot twists, and give you an extra shot for success.

- It's like a bodyguard checking and rechecking the perimeter to make sure the security plan is airtight, as did Frank Farmer, literally, in *The Bodyguard*.
- It's like anonymously publishing the story about the special pie Minny Jackson made for Hilly Holbrook in *The Help*.
- It's like Jess Bhamra becoming so good at soccer, she's awarded a scholarship and wins over her parents' traditional, conservative views in *Bend It Like Beckham*.
- It's like a presenter risking looking ridiculous by overpreparing and practicing in dramatic ways. Oh, wait, that's me.

The amount of time people invest in writing a book or screenplay before it goes to market—and gets published or produced—always surprises me. The unofficial industry average is thirty-three revisions for either type of material. And to write a viable, sellable script takes at minimum two years, maybe three. Certainly, it can take more. Developing any work to a level that makes it marketable is an achievement to be celebrated.

In 2012, I had one such project. It was an action-thriller screenplay that I cowrote, called "Mindgate." The story is about a discharged FBI agent who is given information about a covert government program involving mind-reading technology. This technology is for real, is currently being tested by military and security companies, and will be in use in a few decades. As a result of this information, the agent becomes an assassination target and must work with a super-sharp neuroscientist to go public with the government's subversive plan before they are killed.

By 2012, I had invested three years into the script. Keep in mind that an MFA in screenwriting from a top university is like a gold-embossed lottery ticket. Hitting the jackpot with a script sale is difficult at best, so, like everything in life, you do better when you know the game you're playing. Sixty thousand screenplays are registered with the Writers Guild of America annually, and less than a hundred make it to the big screen each year. This was on the verge of Netflix and before the online distribution boom. In 2011, the script qualified for scouting and got the attention of a producer. I was thrilled. My cowriter and I did another year and a half or so of development work on the script and decided to market it at the highest-recommended pitch festival.

It was my first time pitching. At this event, screenwriters can "buy" five-minute spots with agents and production companies to pitch scripts. At other fests, you'd be in a mosh pit waiting in line for God knows how long. I figured this was our best bet. We reviewed the list of attendees and secured slots with those who made films in our genre—twenty-five in total. Fellow writers told us we were insane to do twenty-five meetings in two days. They each had two to four meetings.

One thing to understand is that this investment, at the very best, is meant to yield a 25 to 30 percent success rate—meaning, if you have the best possible outcome, 25 to 30 percent of the people you meet with will request your script. And there's no guarantee they'll read it, much less buy it. With virtually no contacts in the industry, it was our best shot.

My friend Lee coached us on exactly how to craft our pitch, what to say, what not to say, how to prepare, and how much to rehearse. I did exactly what she said. Every word and every action. But I was still nervous. I thought, *Man, maybe I'm just going to be nervous no matter what.* But I didn't want to feel like a nervous wreck in these meetings. I wanted to feel on top of it. If there was a deal to be had, I needed to know I gave it my all. So I kept rehearsing. Kept refining. Kept preparing.

One day, while rehearsing at Pitfire Pizza on Westwood Boulevard in Los Angeles, I hit the wall. I had the pitch down, but I wasn't gaining confidence in giving it. I was starting to feel bored and like the exercise was not moving the needle any further. I wanted to get to the point at which I knew in my bones I could handle anything that came up during the two days of pitching twenty-five companies.

Then I came up with this idea... bulletproofing.

I made a list of all of the things that an agent or producer could do that would throw me off: interrupt, talk over me, yawn, make weird sounds like constant, low-volume moaning and groaning, lie down on the floor and take a nap, get up and walk away, sing a song, roll his eyes, look bored, check his watch. Then I randomly recruited staff and strangers at Pitfire Pizza, requesting that they behave like total assholes while I ran through the pitch again and again. I finally had to stop because I was laughing too hard, but this crazy idea proved to be the best exercise ever.

Arriving at the pitch fest days later, what would've usually been a nervous and falling apart little me was instead a matador ready to go into the ring. My mindset had totally shifted from an under-the-breath "oh shit" to a roaring "let me outta the gate!!" I was ready. So up we went. Our best chance was to get four to eight requests. We finished with thirteen. Thirteen requests to read "Mindgate" from thirteen of the top production companies and managers in the industry. Double the best possible outcome defined by previous conference-goers. That is why I'm talking about bulletproofing here. It works.

As far as that script... ultimately, we presold it as an indirect result of this effort. It was announced in *Variety* magazine the following year, followed by some opaquely defined rewrite requests for a Chinese investor, denial by the Chinese censorship bureau, a symphony of crickets, and the project fizzling to a coma. It's since been revived and is currently back in play under a new agreement with new players.

The biggest win out of this experience was walking away with the knowledge and exact recipe of how to do this again and again, anytime I want. Careful crafting of your goals is important. Keeping your eye on the prize: critical. Going for what you want using every resource within you: masterful.

At its core, bulletproofing is about protecting your assets.

Your Personal Kevlar

Neutralizers work like Kevlar in a way and can be information, wisdom, rehearsal, allies, mentors or models, or personal strength—whatever protects you from outside forces putting a bullet in your success or helps you overcome any roadblock successfully. You really must prepare for this. In my master class, Carole's goal was to scale her business, using a book and online courses to reach more customers at different places in their journey. However, she found that she had considerable resistance to building a team and leveraging people to support her. She thought of it as cheating. In reality, it was ensuring success and accelerating progress. So, we had to figure out how to address this disconnect.

Carole identified five roadblocks:

- Never written a book before
- Started and stopped many times already
- Don't have a huge social media following
- Don't have a huge email list
- Lots of competition

After doing the critical-thinking exercise with our film mentors (see the exercises at the end of the chapter), Carole identified these as the neutralizers to her roadblocks:

- Got a mentor to help and now can hire a developmental editor (resources)
- Started and stopped college the first time, too; then, when ready, nailed it (resilience)
- Kept plugging away it at and can do the same to grow social media and email (stick-to-itiveness)
- Lost to competition before and got it on the rebound (persistence and resilience)

See how even her tone has a bit more swagger? I love it. "I have the resources, I just have to make use of them," Carole told me.

You remember what else is a resource? Allies. Allies are the universal force multiplier in every real-life story and are usually a key element that pushes the hero to their success and a critical moment. You'll explore this further in the exercises in this chapter. For now, let's look at Megan's story.

Megan has passed two bar exams and published scholarly articles while overcoming panic attacks, fatigue, fearing failure, second-guessing, a lack of confidence, and people with opposing opinions—a cocktail of opposition that could make anyone's head spin. In my master class, she was pursuing her first investment property with her husband so they could build a future. To bulletproof her plans, she focused on the lessons from her past stories and listed them as neutralizers. They would have changed the outcomes for her back then, so she reasoned that she could apply them to her current goal:

- I could have asked for help sooner

- I could have done more to take care of myself so that stress and fatigue did not overcome me

- I could have trusted myself

- I could have accepted failure as a possibility, but with the understanding that without the potential for failure there would be nothing to gain

- I could have tuned out the negative opinions around me sooner

This exercise helped Megan summarize everything she's learned through the exercises up to now. "I noticed that when I dig deep enough, my life stories do actually have similarities to movies, even though my goals and roadblocks might not be as dramatic or intense," Megan said.

Megan's insights provide an important highlight to the exercises in each chapter here that ask you to reflect on the lessons, observations, and insights you have each step of the way. This reflection allows us to anchor in past and current learning so we can apply it forward and expedite results—and also not reinvent the wheel.

Consider this: if your life were a movie, the screenwriter would have each obstacle and how you overcome it figured out by the time the rest of us read the first page. You can do this, too. How can you amplify the forces of your positive attributes? Will your focus on the big picture and drive to succeed overpower someone else's inadvertent attempt at derailment—such as yawning and checking their watch during a pitch?

EXERCISES

1 Review the roadblocks, allies, and strengths for our three iconic characters. How did they neutralize their roadblocks to still achieve success?

   Erin Brockovich
   From broke and jobless to a millionaire legal advocate.

   Roadblocks:

   - Lack of formal education
   - Impatient, unprofessional
   - Gets fired
   - PG&E lawyers; lack of resources
   - Personal life suffers

   Strengths:

   - Smart
   - Resourceful
   - Hard worker
   - Determined
   - Passion for justice

Allies:

- Children
- Ed Masry
- George
- The Jensens; people of Hinkley
- Charles Embry

How Erin neutralized her roadblocks:

1 _____
2 _____
3 _____
4 _____
5 _____

Jason Bourne

From amnesiac to self-actualized.

Roadblocks:

- Suspicion at embassy
- CIA
- Treadstone
- Lack of memory
- Doesn't know who to trust

Strengths:

- Fit
- Determined
- Strong
- Polyglot, a human lethal weapon
- Resourceful

Allies:

- Fishermen
- Marie Kreutz
- Nicolette Parsons
- Marie's ex

How Jason neutralized his roadblocks:

1 _____
2 _____
3 _____
4 _____
5 _____

Akeelah Anderson

From being bullied for smarts to national spelling bee champion.

Roadblocks:

- Lack of resources
- Mom
- Lack of experience/behind other competitors
- Grieving her father
- Lack of family support

Strengths:

- Smart
- Hard worker
- Coachable
- Loyal friend
- Good heart

Allies:

- Her teachers and Principal Welch
- Dr. Larabee
- Javier
- Her mother
- Kiana

How Akeelah neutralized her roadblocks:

1 _____
2 _____
3 _____
4 _____
5 _____

2 List five roadblocks from each of your three success stories. Roadblocks can be weaknesses, flaws, antagonists, or plot twists.

3 Identify the biggest potential roadblocks—anything that could derail you physically, emotionally, intellectually, spiritually, and otherwise—to your current goal.

4 Identify at least one neutralizer for each roadblock for your past stories and current goal. In other words, looking back, what did you do to overcome your roadblock, and looking forward, what could you do?

5 Look back at the work on allies you did in chapter 7. Given that allies are a universal force multiplier for success, I want you to double your allies. In other words, list five more allies

who could potentially help you achieve success. Who would they be and how would they contribute to getting you to your goal?

6   Now stretch further. Go beyond your comfort zone, into the land where Hollywood movie interventions happen and write down what tripling your allies would look like. In other words, imagine, "If I had five more allies, in addition to the ones I already listed, here's who they would be and how they would contribute to my goal."

7   Choose three mindset mantras to get you into a decisive mode, like mine from my grandmother: "Give 'er!" Whatever works for you: write them in your notebook and repeat them on Post-its for your bathroom mirror, underwear drawer, the inside of your tea cabinet door, your fridge, or your wallet. Place each somewhere you will see it often.

8   Record three observations or lessons in your experience with bulletproofing.

Having completed these steps, your inner heroine, along with your action plan, will be bulletproofed. So go out and do your next great thing.

CONCLUSION
YOUR NEXT CALL

• • • • •

"I want you to walk out of here tonight not loving me more, but loving yourselves more."

LADY GAGA

I DID IT: I blew out the motherboard on my panic attacks. I moved the needle. I finished up my point B with the ability to get back into the water panic-free. I wasn't completely over the butterflies and tingles, but I could get in the water, and from there, I knew I could get myself the rest of the way. I could hang out with my niece and nephew in lakes, oceans, and pools. I resumed swimming. I could shower and enjoy soaking tubs. And along with that came a host of other wonderful moments and changes in my life: I moved into a gorgeous penthouse on the ocean, wrote more screenplays, spent time between the Dominican Republic and the United States, auditioned for a band, started a writers group, and did a stint as a guest chocolate chef for a top restaurant. I pivoted my career from corporate work that no longer satisfied me to being a writing coach and developmental editor, which I love. I ate fresh pineapple, sipped cocktails at the beach, explored waterfalls, and made friends from around the world. My life has literally never been the same.

As for my relationship with the water, for a long time, I swam laps in a pool. I've shifted to open-water swimming, and a new wild dream is to help increase the swimming proficiency in the Dominican Republic: an estimated 80 percent of people on the island do not know how to swim. I want to help change that.

If you've applied The Hollywood Approach to your next wildest dream, you, too, may have found that new doors have opened to new adventures, to your next big quest. I hope you will keep going, keep exploring, and keep applying the principles of screenwriting to make your life a masterpiece.

Magnificence and Defiance

Butterflies are magnificent creatures. Universally heralded as a symbol of transformation and hope, we see representations of them everywhere. Logos, themes, memes, tote bags. Purple, blue, pink, orange, and yellow. The real things look as though they smell like flowers. We marvel at their beauty and charm.

That's nice, but it's only part of the narrative. The real story is that butterflies are defiant badasses who perform unbelievable feats barely matched by modern computers. *That's* what the memes and tote bags should say. We're all familiar with the "ugly caterpillar" transformation. But what many people don't realize is that as a caterpillar cocoons itself for ten days, it's basically melting itself in acid as many as four times. Then, it emerges as a butterfly with wet wings. And as soon as its wings dry, the magnificent creature is able to fly. Just like that.

This is not to imply that butterflies are perfect. They have flaws, too. They can fly only in ideal conditions, so: no flying when it's hot; no flying when it's wet; and no flying when it's windy.

Monarchs, for example, make a colossal two-thousand-mile journey from the Canadian ice belt to a particular village in Mexico. The third or fourth generation arrives on the Day of the Dead, every year, numbering in the millions.

Scientists cannot fully explain it. But butterflies make it work because they maximize their strengths—just like action heroines.

And real-life heroines! We are all butterflies in our own way, maximizing the things that work for us to achieve incredible things. Even if no one can officially verify how butterflies perform their awe-inspiring exploits, everyone knows this: a butterfly never turns back into a caterpillar.

And neither will you.

Captivate Yourself

It's time to leverage your Story MBA—remember, we talked about you having twelve master's degrees in story consumption if you're running about average and have been watching TV since 1995. You are a sophisticated story consumer, primed to leverage what you've learned in this book. Light up all seven areas of your brain and get your oxytocin and dopamine flowing. Fly in your ideal conditions. Become re-enchanted with your story. It's the greatest healing art you have.

Like I did, at 27 Waterfalls.

Like Bill did, wherever he is—hopefully playing Fleetwood Mac songs, maybe *with* Fleetwood Mac.

Like Annie, who proved that analyzing your character DNA can propel you forward.

Like Anne, the cancer-surviving Texas debutante who is now happily married to a former Olympic javelin thrower. Together, they adopted three orphaned brothers. She lives in a house of men and continues to script and reenact hilarious victories for humankind daily.

Like Jessica, the crafty prescription artist, who is fully back on her feet and living fiercely.

Like Kendra, for whom everyone is holding their breath while she finishes her book about her casino days. In the meantime, she has a top restaurant in the Caribbean and has begun franchising it.

Like Tom, who is working on the other six summits.

Like Jason, whose corporate life is fading in the rearview as his coaching business takes off.

Like Sharon, whose finances are in order as she faces her next chapter.

Like Sheila, who finished the exercises with a new level of clarity she didn't know she needed, launched a new rainmaking business model, and rocks it poolside from Mexico.

Like Francesca, who got clear on her resistance and self-sabotage. With the information she needed, she has started a writing class. I look forward to her book!

Like Tasha, whose culinary yoga retreat in Marrakech took off to rave reviews with guests calling it "over-the-top wonderful."

You don't need vision boards and twenty thousand apps. You need to work like the master you are to parlay your Story MBA, to say "hell, yes!" to the ride of your life, to live your next wildest dream. You have gone through a more rigorous set of exercises than some Hollywood screenwriters do when writing a feature protagonist, and you've done it for the most powerful heroine in your life: you. I am bursting with excitement for you, because I've seen what these insights can do firsthand.

If you have invested in the work, it has likely led you to more certainty, strength, and confidence in yourself—about who you are, what you're made of, and what's possible for you. There is so much magic to be had in the world. Even amid a shitstorm, there is beauty in finding previously untapped courage and rising up to be everything you are meant to be in this moment. Because before you know it, the moment can turn into your life.

I hope you will take each tool and leap tall obstacles in a single bound. Fly high wherever you need to go. Stop bullets with your golden cuffs. Use the lasso of truth on yourself. Remember, truth and certainty will always move your story forward. Recalling your SMART goal from chapter 2, reflect for a moment on the measurable difference you have experienced. What milestones have you already achieved? What changes have you made? What chances have you taken? What victories have you attained? Every step, no matter how small, is an achievement, for we know that tiny steps lead to small steps, which lead to little and big things as you shift the trajectory of your entire life. It's really something to marvel at. Being able to reflect on your past success stories through the same construct as you go after your next successes allows you to put them on a level playing field next to iconic characters such as those listed in this book, as well as all characters from every corner of the world.

You are your own hero. And you're ready to prove it over and over again. I cannot wait to see and hear about what has become possible for you through this work. These tools are always accessible to you, and since this combines visualization with clear icons and action, it will always work—when you do the work.

I hope you take the leap into each and every one of your next wildest dreams.

ACKNOWLEDGMENTS

WRITING IS A team sport, and I'm very grateful to all of the people who brought their A game to my arena.

The people of Cabarete, for making this a magical place.

Jill Paider, for your vision in seeing this as a book and pulling it out of me as only a sister can.

Bobby Z and Bobby C, for forever changing the trajectory of my story.

Robert Powell, for your mentorship, camaraderie, and superior badassery. Your leadership evoked profound healing and transformation.

Mom, for teaching me the love of language, reading, writing, and vocabulary, and Dad, for the creative usage of it.

Verna and Louis Johnson, for guiding the way.

AJ Harper, for raising your hand to be on my editorial team no more than nine seconds after I told you about this project.

Laura Stone, for being the best wing-woman a woman could hope for. Leather Tuscadero has nothing on you.

I am also grateful to these amazing places and people and teams: andBeyond Ngorongoro Crater Lodge in Tanzania, where this idea was first transformed into manuscript format; my adopted families and homes away from home in Arizona—Terri

Clubb and The Clubb House and Lisa P and the LP Roadhouse; Inn at Nye Beach, a great place for writing on the Oregon coast; the Millennium Resort & Spa in Cabarete; and Andari Spa, Claro, VoyVoy, Fresh Fresh, Front Loop, and Gorditos, with much reverence; my deepest gratitude for your hospitality, friendship, and support.

To each person who leaned forward when they heard this idea: my master class students, interviewees, my Cabarete book club, my colleagues at Convince & Convert, and the wonderful team of amazing collaborators at Page Two. Thank you for being my force multipliers in making this vision a reality.

And finally, to every underdog everywhere: choose love.

SELECTED SOURCES

THE FOLLOWING is a selection of key sources referred to in the chapters.

Introduction: The Call to Adventure

Avildsen, John G., dir. *Rocky.* 1976; film. Philadelphia, PA: United Artists.

Campbell, Gavin James. "'The Outer Limits of Probability': A Janis Joplin Retrospective." *Southern Cultures* 6, no. 3 (2000). doi.org/10.1353/scu.2000.0040.

DuVernay, Ava, dir. *A Wrinkle in Time.* 2018; film. Los Angeles, CA: Legend3D.

Favreau, Jon, dir. *Iron Man.* 2008; film. Palmdale, CA: Paramount Pictures.

Feig, Paul, dir. *Ghostbusters.* 2016; film. Boston, MA: Columbia Pictures.

Fleming, Victor, dir. *The Wizard of Oz.* 1939; film. Culver City, CA: Warner Bros.

Jenkins, Patty, dir. *Wonder Woman.* 2017; film. London, England: Warner Bros.

Raimi, Sam, dir. *Spider-Man.* 2002; film. Valhalla, NY: Columbia Pictures.

Ross, Gary, dir. *Ocean's 8*. 2018; film. New York, NY: Warner Bros.

Wan, James, dir. *Aquaman*. 2018; film. Queensland, AU: DC Comics.

1 Be Your Own Hero

Atchison, Doug, dir. *Akeelah and the Bee*. 2006; film. Santa Monica, CA: Lionsgate.

Liman, Doug, dir. *The Bourne Identity*. 2002; film. Universal City, CA: Universal Pictures.

Ramirez, Erica. "Beyoncé Takes Fans Behind the Scenes on MTV Special." *Billboard,* July 1, 2011. billboard.com/articles/columns/the-juice/469401/beyonce-takes-fans-behind-the-scenes-on-mtv-special/.

Rampton, John. "Neuroscience Tells Us How to Hack Our Brains for Success." *Entrepreneur,* June 16, 2017. entrepreneur.com/article/295885.

Smith, John N., dir. *Dangerous Minds*. 1995; film. Burbank, CA: Buena Vista Pictures.

Soderbergh, Steven, dir. *Erin Brockovich*. 2000; film. Universal City, CA: Universal Pictures.

Stevens, Susan, and Wayne A. Henning. "Sleep and Wakefulness." In *Textbook of Clinical Neurology*, edited by Christopher G. Goetz, 21–33. Chicago, IL: Saunders, 2007.

2 Your First Big Yes

Biography. S.v. "Amelia Earhart." biography.com/explorer/amelia-earhart.

Cron, Lisa. *Wired for Story: The Writer's Guide to Using Brain Science to Hook Readers from the Very First Sentence.* New York, NY: Ten Speed Press, 2012.
Farrelly, Peter, dir. *Green Book.* 2018; film. New York, NY: Participant.
Landis, John, dir. *Coming to America.* 1988; film. Brooklyn, NY: Paramount Pictures.
Lee, Spike, dir. *BlacKkKlansman.* 2018; film. Ossining, NY: Focus Features.
Liman, Doug, dir. *Fair Game.* 2010; film. Kuala Lumpur, Malaysia: River Road Entertainment.
Luketic, Robert, dir. *Legally Blonde.* 2001; film. Sierra Madre, CA: MGM.
Nair, Mira, dir. *Amelia.* 2009; film. Century City, CA: Fox Searchlight Pictures.
Petrie, Donald, dir. *The Associate.* 1996; film. Long Island, NY: Hollywood Pictures.
Rihanna (@Rihanna). "If you don't live your life, who the fuck will?" Twitter, home page profile picture. twitter.com/irihhanna/.
Ruben, Joseph, dir. *Sleeping with the Enemy.* 1991; film. Abbeville, SC: Twentieth Century Fox.
Scott, Ridley, dir. *Thelma & Louise.* 1991; film. Derby Acres, CA: Pathé Entertainment.

3 Your Narrative Forensics

"100 Women of the Year. 1960: The Mirabal Sisters." *Time*, March 5, 2020. time.com/5793594/mirabal-sisters-100-women-of-the-year/.

Avildsen, John G., dir. *The Karate Kid.* 1984; film. Hollywood, CA: Columbia Pictures.

Barr, Sabrina. "Tina Turner at 80: 17 of the Star's Most Empowering Quotes." *Independent,* November 25, 2019. independent.co.uk/life-style/women/tina-turner-birthday-80-empowering-quotes-inspirational-singer-a9217301.html/.

Barraclough, Leo. "Television Stays Youthful Buoyed by New Distribution Methods and Content, Eurodata Report Shows." *Variety,* April 9, 2018. variety.com/2018/tv/global/tv-consumption-steady-new-distribution-content-eurodata-report-1202747345/.

Barroso, Mariano, dir. *In the Time of the Butterflies.* 2001; film. Beverly Hills, CA: MGM.

Hughes, John, dir. *Ferris Bueller's Day Off.* 1986; film. Chicago, IL: Paramount Pictures.

Lang, Jamie. "Eurodata TV Worldwide Dissects 'One Television Year in the World.'" *Variety,* April 11, 2019. variety.com/2019/tv/festivals/eurodata-tv-worldwide-dissects-one-television-year-in-the-world-1203186715/.

McQueen, Steve, dir. *Widows.* 2018; film. Chicago, IL: Regency Enterprises.

Mendes, Sam, dir. *Skyfall.* 2010: film. London, England: MGM.

Murphy, Ryan, dir. *Eat Pray Love.* 2010; film. Culver City, CA: Columbia Pictures.

Ross, Gary, dir. *The Hunger Games.* 2012; film. Black Mountain, NC: Lionsgate.

Washington, Denzel, dir. *The Great Debaters.* 2007; film. Marshall, TX: Harpo Films.

4 Character DNA Part I: Strengths and Assets

Arrien, Angelis. *Gathering Medicine: Stories, Songs, and Methods for Soul Retrieval*. Performed in front of a live audience by Angelis Arrien. Louisville, CO; Sounds True, 2006; CD.

Kondracki, Larysa, dir. *The Whistleblower*. 2010; film. New York, NY: Samuel Goldwyn Films.

Stolworthy, Jacob, and Clarisse Loughrey. "Madonna at 60: 20 of the Best Quotes from the Queen of Pop." *Independent*, August 16, 2018. independent.co.uk/arts-entertainment/music/features/madonna-best-famous-quotes-sixty-birthday-pop-feminism-sex-religion-fame-a8493781.html/.

5 Character DNA Part II: Amnesia and Superpowers

Haven, Kendall. *Story Proof: The Science behind the Startling Power of Story*. Westport, CT: Libraries Unlimited, 2007.

Melfi, Theodore, dir. *Hidden Figures*. 2016; film. Los Angeles, CA: 20th Century Fox.

Parton, Dolly (@DollyParton). "A peacock who rests on its feathers is just another turkey." Twitter. June 1, 2010, 11:05 a.m. twitter.com/dollyparton/status/15183715134?lang=en/.

Quigley, Elizabeth. "Parkinson's Smell Test Explained by Science." BBC News Scotland, March 20, 2019. bbc.com/news/uk-scotland-47627179.

6 Character DNA Part III: Flawesomeness

Kearney, Laila. "U.S. Plastic Surgery, Cosmetic Spending Hits Record $15 Billion." Reuters, March 15, 2017. reuters.com/article/us-usa-plasticsurgery-idUSKBN16M3BI.

Ladegaard, Isak. "Mental Health Problems Worsen with Cosmetic Surgery." *Science Norway*, July 4, 2012. sciencenorway.no/cosmetics-forskningno-norway/mental-health-problems-worsen-with-cosmetic-surgery/1373674.

Lizzo. "Self-Care Has to Be Rooted in Self-Preservation, Not Just Mimosas and Spa Days." NBC News, April 19, 2019. nbcnews.com/think/opinion/self-care-has-be-rooted-self-preservation-not-just-mimosas-ncna993661/.

Russell, David O., dir. *Joy*. 2015; film. Los Angeles, CA: 20th Century Fox.

Smith, Sophia. "The Japanese Art of Recognizing Beauty in Broken Things." *Makezine*, July 17, 2015. makezine.com/2015/08/17/kintsugi-japanese-art-recognizing-beauty-broken-things/.

7 Allies: The Force Multiplier

Berkoff, Marc. "The Importance of Play: Having Fun Must Be Taken Seriously." *Psychology Today*, May 2, 2014. psychologytoday.com/au/blog/animal-emotions/201405/the-importance-play-having-fun-must-be-taken-seriously.

Brown, Stuart, with Christopher Vaughan. *Play: How It Shapes the Brain, Opens the Imagination, and Invigorates the Soul*. New York, NY: Avery, 2009.

Kwapis, Ken, dir. *Big Miracle*. 2012; film. Universal City, CA: Universal Pictures.

Locke, Ashley. "30 Diana Ross Quotes That'll Inspire You for Years and Years." Women.com, April 16, 2020. women.com/ashleylocke/lists/diana-ross-quotes-071019/.

Peña, Laura. Interviews with the author, July 20, 2018, June 4, 2019, and November 18, 2019.

Punkoney, Sarah. "Play and How It Impacts Early Brain Development." Stay at Home Educator, June 17, 2012. stayathomeeducator.com/play-impacts-early-brain-development/.

8 Drink Your Antagonists' Tears

"Anti-gay Pastor May Lose Church to LGBT Group." Edited and produced by Drew Katchen. MSNBC Originals, April 13, 2016. Video, 4:54. msnbc.com/msnbc-quick-cuts/watch/anti-gay-pastor-may-lose-church-to-lgbt-group-665170499526.

Chu, Jon M., dir. *Crazy Rich Asians*. 2018; film. Burbank, CA: Warner Bros. Pictures.

Fairbanks, Sammie. "18 Times Taylor Swift, Only a High School Grad, Unintentionally Described College Perfectly." *Odyssey*, April 16, 2018. theodysseyonline.com/best-taylor-swift-quotes/.

Hawkins, David R. *Power vs. Force: The Hidden Determinants of Human Behavior*. Sedona, AZ: Veritas, 1995.

Siciliano, Carl. Interview with the author, February 21, 2020.

9 Mentors and Models

"8 Benefits of Starting a Mentor Program at Your Company." Frontier Business, October 21, 2016. business.frontier.com/blog/8-benefits-of-starting-a-mentor-program-at-your-company/.

Bourdeau, Michelle. Interview with the author, March 10, 2020.

Bronzite, Dan. "The Hero's Journey: Mythic Structure of Joseph Campbell's Monomyth." Movie Outline. movieoutline.com/articles/the-hero-journey-mythic-structure-of-joseph-campbell-monomyth.html.

Lawrence, Tom. Interview with the author, November 2, 2018.

Mallett, Ryan. "Imagery and Visualization: Strength and Conditioning for the Athletic Brain." BelievePerform. believeperform.com/imagery-and-visualization-strength-and-conditioning-for-the-athletic-brain/.

Meah, Asad. "40 Inspirational Jennifer Hudson Quotes on Success." Awaken the Greatness Within. awakenthegreatnesswithin.com/40-inspirational-jennifer-hudson-quotes-on-success/.

Winfrey, Oprah. USC Annenberg Commencement Speech. May 11, 2018. YouTube video, 23:15. youtube.com/watch?v=7Sip6xy1kIk.

Wise, Robert, dir. *The Sound of Music*. 1965; film. Los Angeles, CA: 20th Century Fox.

10 Annnnnd... Action

"16 Adele Quotes That Will Make You Love Who You Are." Goalcast, July 11, 2017. goalcast.com/2017/07/11/adele-quotes-love-who-you-are/.

Earle, Christal. Interview with the author, January 12, 2020.

Gilbert, Megan. "Living a Life in 100 Miles." *Extra Ordinary*, January 21, 2019. Podcast, 25:02. stitcher.com/podcast/mg-productions/extra-ordinary-2.

Popova, Maria. "Martha Graham on the Life-Force of Creativity and the Divine Dissatisfaction of Being an Artist." *Brain Pickings*, October 2, 2015. brainpickings.org/2015/10/02/martha-graham-creativity-divine-dissatisfaction/.

Scafaria, Lorene, dir. *Hustlers*. 2019; film. Burbank, CA: STX Entertainment.

11 Plot Twists and the Dark Night of the Soul

Finley, Taryn. "9 Quotes from Queen Latifah That Remind Us She's a Literal Queen." *Huffington Post,* March 18, 2016. huffpost.com/entry/9-quotes-from-queen-latifah-that-remind-us-shes-a-literal-queen_n_56eae173e4b03a640a69cd8f/.

Mariposa Foundation (@DRMariposas). "Happy birthday to our honorary chairwoman and inspiration to us all, Julia Alvarez! Julia's kindness and humility ring true in her own words, 'You aren't what you accomplish, you are what you overcome.'" Twitter, March 27, 2020, 8:17 a.m. twitter.com/DRMariposas/status/1243512587326717954.

Nair, Mira, dir. *Queen of Katwe*. 2016; film. Burbank, CA: Walt Disney Studios Motion Pictures.

12 The Supreme Ordeal

Berg, Brenda. "How to Use the Power of the Subconscious Mind to Succeed." Management30, April 10, 2018. management30.com/blog/subconscious-success/.

Dooley, Roger. "Brain Decides, Then Tells You Later." Neuromarketing. neurosciencemarketing.com/blog/articles/subconscious-decision.htm.

Levin, Marissa. "How to Avoid the 3 Most Dangerous Roles in Leadership (and Life)." *Inc.*, September 8, 2016. inc.com/marissa-levin/the-three-most-dangerous-roles-in-life-and-leadership-and-how-to-avoid-them.html.

"Measurement Methods." Master Mindo. mapofspirituality.org/measurement-methods/.

Roach, Jay, dir. *Bombshell*. 2019; film. Santa Monica, CA: Lionsgate.

Rocío González Soto, Fernanda. Interviews with the author, February 17, 2020 (Mara Fernandez translator) and January 14, 2020 (Vanessa Porro translator).

Sheth, Bhavin, et al. "Posterior Beta and Anterior Gamma Oscillations Predict Cognitive Insight." *Journal of Cognitive Neuroscience* 21, no. 7 (2009). doi.org/10.1162/jocn.2009.21069.

Wareing, Charlotte. "Jennifer Lopez Reveals How Actor Ben Affleck Was Her 'First Big Heartbreak.'" *Irish Mirror*, November 1, 2014. irishmirror.ie/showbiz/celebrity-news/jennifer-lopez-reveals-how-actor-4550007/.

13 Love Conquers All

Angelo, Gail. Interview with the author, April 24, 2020.

Cassavetes, Nick, dir. *The Notebook*. 2004; film. Los Angeles, CA: New Line Cinema.

Lasher, Megan. "10 Cher Quotes That Will Make You Feel Like Anything Is Possible." *Time*, May 20, 2016. time.com/4336945/cher-quotes-birthday/.

"A Letter from Albert Einstein to His Daughter: On the Universal Force of Love," Monoset. monoset.com/blogs/journal/a-letter-from-albert-einstein-to-his-daughter-on-the-universal-force-of-love.

McNamara, Sean, dir. *Soul Surfer*. 2011; film. Kauai, HI: TriStar Pictures.

14 Bulletproofing

Chadha, Gurinder, dir. *Bend It Like Beckham*. 2002; film. Middlesex, England: Kintop Pictures.

Encyclopaedia Britannica. S.v. "Ruth Bader Ginsberg." Updated March 11, 2020. britannica.com/biography/Ruth-Bader-Ginsburg.

Jackson, Mick, dir. *The Bodyguard*. 1992; film. Beverly Hills, CA: Kasdan Pictures.

Leder, Mimi, dir. *On the Basis of Sex*. 2018; film. New York, NY: Focus Features.

Maloney, Maggie. "Aretha Franklin's Most Iconic Quotes of All Time." *Town and Country*, August 16, 2018. townandcountrymag.com/leisure/arts-and-culture/a22713964/aretha-franklin-quotes/.

Oyez. S.v. "Ruth Bader Ginsberg." oyez.org/justices/ruth_bader_ginsburg.

Taylor, Tate, dir. *The Help*. 2011; film. Clarksdale, MS: DreamWorks.

Zeldin, Noel. Interview with the author, April 29, 2019.

Conclusion: Your Next Call

Gaga, Lady. "I want you to walk out of here tonight not loving me more, but loving yourselves more." Goodreads. goodreads.com/quotes/294513-i-want-you-to-walk-out-of-here-tonight-not.

PHOTO COURTESY OF DAVID LEE

www.ingramcontent.com/pod-product-compliance
Lightning Source LLC
Chambersburg PA
CBHW021440070526
44577CB00002B/222

ABOUT KRISTINA PAIDER

A **SCREENWRITER AND STORY** strategist, Kristina Paider has moved from newsrooms to boardrooms to Hollywood writers' rooms as a sought-after collaborator on high-performance teams in thirty-four countries. She has practiced The Hollywood Approach for two decades, helping people and companies live their best story.

For workshops, master classes, or what's new, visit
KRISTINAPAIDER.COM